Philosophy and the Metaphysical Achievements of Education

Philosophy and the Metaphysical Achievements of Education

Language and Reason

Ryan McInerney

BLOOMSBURY ACADEMIC
LONDON • NEW YORK • OXFORD • NEW DELHI • SYDNEY

BLOOMSBURY ACADEMIC
Bloomsbury Publishing Plc
50 Bedford Square, London, WC1B 3DP, UK
1385 Broadway, New York, NY 10018, USA
29 Earlsfort Terrace, Dublin 2, Ireland

BLOOMSBURY, BLOOMSBURY ACADEMIC and the Diana logo
are trademarks of Bloomsbury Publishing Plc

First published in Great Britain 2021
This paperback edition published 2023

Copyright © Ryan McInerney, 2021

Ryan McInerney has asserted his right under the Copyright, Designs
and Patents Act, 1988, to be identified as Author of this work.

Cover design: Charlotte Daniels
Cover image © Baivector/Shutterstock

All rights reserved. No part of this publication may be reproduced or transmitted in
any form or by any means, electronic or mechanical, including photocopying,
recording, or any information storage or retrieval system, without prior
permission in writing from the publishers.

Bloomsbury Publishing Plc does not have any control over, or responsibility for,
any third-party websites referred to or in this book. All internet addresses given in
this book were correct at the time of going to press. The author and publisher
regret any inconvenience caused if addresses have changed or sites have
ceased to exist, but can accept no responsibility for any such changes.

A catalogue record for this book is available from the British Library.

Library of Congress Cataloging-in-Publication Data
Names: McInerney, Ryan, author.
Title: Philosophy and the metaphysical achievements of education :
language and reason / Ryan McInerney.
Description: New York, NY : Bloomsbury Academic, 2021. | Includes
bibliographical references and index. |
Identifiers: LCCN 2021000347 (print) | LCCN 2021000348 (ebook) |
ISBN 9781350183513 (hardback) | ISBN 9781350183520 (ebook) |
ISBN 9781350183537 (epub)
Subjects: LCSH: Education–Philosophy. | Education–Aims and objectives. |
Metaphysics. | Language and languages–Philosophy.
Classification: LCC LB14.7 .M38 2021 (print) | LCC LB14.7 (ebook) | DDC 370.1–dc23
LC record available at https://lccn.loc.gov/2021000347
LC ebook record available at https://lccn.loc.gov/2021000348

ISBN: HB: 978-1-3501-8351-3
PB: 978-1-3501-8518-0
ePDF: 978-1-3501-8352-0
ePUB: 978-1-3501-8353-7

Typeset by Integra Software Services Pvt. Ltd.

To find out more about our authors and books visit www.bloomsbury.com
and sign up for our newsletters.

For Atlas and André

I am grateful to the Social Sciences and Humanities Research Council of Canada for its support of my research.

Contents

Preface	x
Overture: What Are Philosophical Theses?	1
1 Education and Philosophy: A Crisis of Self-Identity	9
2 Education and Metaphysics: Being at Home in the World	39
3 Education and History: Out into the Midst of Being	63
4 The Structure of Educational Ideals: Transcendental Origins, Impossible Aims	87
5 Education and Transcendence: At Home in *Unheimlich* Language	111
Coda: Waking Thinking Being	135
References	141
Index	151

Preface

This book is one result of my personal struggle with the experience of education broadly conceived—that is, of becoming a thinking being—and with the utter lack of honest and open reflection, both public and private, about what that amounts to. It was only after reading David Bakhurst's *The Formation of Reason* that the real possibility of undertaking an academic project of this scope emerged. It seemed, at first, a salutary happenstance that the philosophy of education provides the conceptual space to confront such broad ideas, but it quickly became clear that this is no accident, and a significant portion of this book is dedicated to explaining why. In doing so, I hope to have indicated something of the monumental importance of education as a human undertaking and of philosophical reflection concerning it. The extent to which I have failed or succeeded in providing an opportunity for the reader to contemplate these ideas in an impassioned but serious manner remains to be seen.

I want to appreciate every teacher, student, family member, and friend who has contributed to my learning experience, and I want to say that their influences speak through me in these chapters as a kind of dynamic totality of my own unfinished education. I can here attempt only a meager but heartfelt thanks to some of them. Three teachers deserve mention: John Loewen, from whom I learned the seriousness in life and study that caused me to pursue philosophy in the first place; Scott Pound, my undergraduate English professor who has since become a close friend and fishing partner; and my first philosophy teacher, Tony Larivière, who has been an exacting mentor and magnificent host. I am also thankful to the following friends and family, in no particular order, for challenging and supporting my endeavors: Clay Breiland, Matt and Riley St. Hilaire, Tim Stevenson, Ray Timmerman, Dave Thebault, the Hettinga family, Aaron and the Gens family, and the Beckels.

I owe special thanks to David Bakhurst, my graduate supervisor, for his patience, guidance, and wisdom. He is the most philosophically dexterous person I have met, and his work has greatly inspired my own. I am also grateful to Paul Standish for his insight and hospitality during my studies in the UK.

Helping put this project into perspective and motivating its completion has been the vivid memory of my intelligent, kind, and patient mother, Johanne, who passed away almost exactly a year ago. I love her very much and I miss her deeply. It has become clear that her death has impelled a sense of daring, for myself and my brilliant siblings, Shauna and James, to challenge ourselves and each other to live our dreams. They know all about the gratitude they deserve.

I dedicate this book to my beautiful young sons, Atlas and André, who I hope will someday encounter a familiar mind in these pages. There are, however, two other people whose positive influence on my life and work it would be difficult to overstate. The first is my father, Michael, a teacher whose educative methods and especially whose thirst for learning I always continue to appreciate. He has been the most unwavering supporter of everything I have ever tried to accomplish. The other great influence is the love of my life, my wonderful Sarah. She is also a teacher whose virtuous effects on her students and colleagues she would never admit. She is astoundingly kind and a brilliant, dedicated mother to our children, but her straightforward commitment to honesty and goodness is what, for me, sets her apart from the rest of the world. I am grateful to her for the unlimited patience, faithfulness, and benevolence that she bestows upon me and those around her. I love her completely.

I hope the reader finds within this book the marks of honest thinking. Some of it will resemble frantic speculation, lyricism, and metaphor; some of it will resemble sober argumentation; some of it will resemble a mélange of favored passages and turns of phrase emanating from preferred philosophers. Although various portions of the text may be vexatious to some readers, I have tried in good faith to offer something of value to everyone. In my view, philosophy is a personal journey of the highest adventure and a fundamental demand of human life that is the very effect of education universally. I hope the idiosyncrasies that constitute this work do not discourage the reader from seriously considering that broad idea from an equally personal standpoint.

Lake of the Woods, Canada
November 2020

Overture: What Are Philosophical Theses?

This book addresses the basic aims and achievements of education. It recognizes language as central to thinking, and philosophy and education as belonging profoundly to one another. In this brief introduction, I invite the careful reader by articulating, in bold terms, some key refrains of the chapters to follow.

Philosophical thinking begins to understand itself when it remembers the untiring universality of language, but such acts of remembering are like arriving at an endless beginning. To think this is to venture beyond Ludwig Wittgenstein's quietist announcement in the *Investigations*: "If one tried to advance *theses* in philosophy, it would never be possible to debate them, because everyone would agree to them" (1958: §128; original italics). We must venture beyond this because, although it is true that "[p]hilosophy puts everything before us," it cannot honestly imagine itself doing so in such a way that "everything lies open to view," as Wittgenstein says it does (§126). Hans-Georg Gadamer's idea, for example, that all understanding and misunderstanding presupposes "a deep common accord" (1966b: 7) is supposed to be part of the accord itself—a philosophical thesis to which everyone, including Wittgenstein, might agree. What, though, does such a thesis actually say? It does not present a tantalizing philosophical problem in the traditional sense, but mere agreement falls radically short here: for having heard the phrase "deep common accord" we can hardly return to the rough ground of living without wondering what it is all of us already agree so deeply, or what it could possibly mean to partake in such universal communion. To what extent, then, is there "nothing to explain" (Wittgenstein 1958: §126)?

"The results of philosophy," as Wittgenstein would have it, "are the uncovering of one or another piece of plain nonsense" (§119) so that we can "*command a clear view* of the use of our words" (§122; original italics). He acknowledges that such investigating "seems only to destroy everything interesting" (§118)—in particular, the purported "*depth*" of philosophical "disquietudes" (§111; original italics)—but this is what should give the philosopher "peace" (§133). It is the work of philosophy instead to resist its own affinity for nonsense by pointing out how ostensibly deep philosophical puzzles merely contravene those rules of ordinary meaning by which, once disclosed, "we fail to be struck" (§129). For Wittgenstein, that is the valuably therapeutic, but not really profound, effect of bringing "words back from their metaphysical to their everyday use" (§116).

How do we challenge Wittgenstein's claim in the following study, and how do we venture beyond it in hopes of recovering the value of philosophical theses, even though we follow Wittgenstein in so many other ways? We challenge it by asking what constitutes a clear view of language. If the answer is supposed to be that our view of language is clear when it is clear of philosophical misunderstandings (cf. §133), that would betray a built-in but ultimately unsupported mistrust of philosophy's honest inquiry into things. The mistrust is understandable generally, in light of philosophy's long history of failure and self-doubt; and it is particularly understandable in view of Wittgenstein's own acknowledged bewitchments (cf. §§109, 114); but does the risk of failure really preclude sincere philosophical inquiry, of the kind that would result, authentically, in "seeing connexions" (§122)? Is it not possible that the "misinterpretation of our forms of language" (§111) and the acknowledgment of that misinterpretation together point the way to a better, more profound, but never ultimate, interpretation? Does this not suggest the symbiosis and mutual presupposition of interpretation and misinterpretation, truth and falsity, clarity and obscurity, presence and difference, health and sickness, trust and mistrust, coda and overture? Contrast with Wittgenstein's rebuke the words of an "ecstatic witness" (Gadamer 1966b: 6) to the transformative power and profound risk-taking of philosophy:

> Life—that means for us constantly transforming all that we are into light and flame—also everything that wounds us; we simply can do no other. And as for sickness: are we not almost tempted to ask whether we can get along without it? ... Only great pain, the long, slow pain that takes its time—on which we are burned, as it were, with green wood—compels us philosophers to descend into our ultimate depths and to put aside all trust. ... I doubt that such pain makes us "better"; but I know that it makes us more *profound*. ... [O]ut of such long and dangerous exercises of self-mastery one emerges as a different person, with a few more question marks—above all with the *will* henceforth to question further, more deeply, severely, harshly, evilly and quietly than one had questioned heretofore.
>
> (Nietzsche 1974: 36; original italics)

Wittgenstein claims that insisting on the depth of philosophical theses about ourselves and the world is misguided, because "one is merely tracing round the frame through which we look at it" (1958: §114). That species of activity, however, is not so different from Immanuel Kant's transcendental undertaking: whereas Kant is "merely tracing" the preconditions of experience, Wittgenstein is "merely tracing" the preconditions of meaning, and we might say too that Gadamer is "merely tracing" the preconditions of understanding;[1] but what those preconditions are; or what they might mean for us in the here and now, remains far from clear. Kant might agree with Wittgenstein's view that what remains truly hidden "is of no interest to us" (1958: §126), but surely it is no mere philosophical malady to be struck by the revelation of things that had for so long remained "hidden because of their simplicity and familiarity. (One is unable to notice something—because it is always before one's eyes.)" (§129) What is perhaps more striking is the unexpected way in which such revealing can transform our view of what is already there and so does not "in the end only describe it" (§124). Although we must admit that it "cannot give [language] any foundation," we need not assent to the further claim that philosophy, in discovering what was previously hidden, "leaves everything as it is" (§124). That is because, as I hope will emerge in this study, philosophy remains part of what is being described and transforms what is described in describing it. Language's self-reflection is not a closed loop, but an open one; and that is due to its untiring universality. The question is whether we dare answer its call.

Where, then, do we find ourselves beginning endlessly, if we venture beyond Wittgenstein's quietism concerning philosophical theses? My suggestion is "philosophy puts everything before us" just by orienting us explicitly to reality at large, the home of thinking beings: it does that, however, from the historical standpoint of language, the medium of thought; and its sayings, which continue to speak through us again and anew, are only ever on the verge of being understood. This orientation, meanwhile, is the original, monumental achievement of education everywhere. Education effects a metaphysical transformation by introducing us to language, the repository of historical mind, and the fount of reason. It introduces us to ourselves as thinking beings and, at the same time, leads us out into the universe as such. Education and philosophy are therefore interested, fundamentally, in "the same"—bare universality, or the transcendence of Being—that "deep common accord" whose understanding is always on the threshold, transformatively, in language.

Philosophy as Responsive, Rudimentary Thinking

Such theses about education, metaphysics, language, and reason are unabashedly philosophical, and they do so much as pretend to have the character of depth. My hope, however, is that the reader understands the following chapters according to the very shape of philosophical understanding that is their recommendation: that is, as a self-consciously historical orientation to language that, while claiming to say something fundamental, nevertheless stands basically and creatively open to question; and not as the formulation of a system built from first principles or in pursuit of the final analysis of concepts. This study is therefore an attempt to say in form what it says directly: it recognizes itself as a mere beginning-to-think and beginning-to-say, a "strategy without finality" (Derrida 2004: 282)—but not without forethought.

A way to introduce the shape of philosophical understanding I am recommending is to revisit the very idea of a "thesis" according to its historical meaning. The core contemporary sense of "thesis" is of a contention requiring proof or, alternatively, defense from impending attack. That, though, is relatively recent, appearing within the last five or six centuries.[2] The Greek *thesis* does mean "proposition," but it also means "down beat" as applied to rhythm—that is, less "contention" than "motif." The latter sense is where the English term "theme" derives its principal meaning of an all-embracing subject or idea: the words "thesis" and "theme" share etymological roots in the Greek *tithenai* (set down, place, arrange, deposit, situate).

Those roots evoke the spirit of music and invite reflection in this vein. When we make music, we cultivate an ongoing theme: we observe a cadence, and we stress particular syllables and notes; we do this in order to situate ourselves in and maintain our common orientation to some bits of rhythm and harmony—an arrangement, a musical accord. Developing a "thesis" in this context is not about ending what has come before only to begin from nowhere; nor is it about attempting to play the lead or distract from the original tune; nor is it about claiming to have discovered the eternally resolving melody of the spheres. It is simply to take up the rhythm and harmony of whatever is already being played, respecting the song's own natural movements and intricacies, so that we can begin again in our exploration of the same musical idea. It is an interpretation, an intelligent response to what is already there. "Only because the text calls for it does interpretation take place, and only in the way called for. The apparently thetic beginning of interpretation is, in fact, a response; and the sense of an interpretation is determined, like every response, by the question asked" (Gadamer 2004b: 467). Philosophical inquiry need not be, and empirically is not, the assertion *ex nihilo* of a first philosophy. We might, with Stanley Cavell, conceive philosophy not "as a kind of writing … but as a kind of reading, say a kind of responsiveness, a kind that understands itself to be endless" (2012a: 32). Philosophy responds by keeping time to what is.

To compress the musical metaphor into a somewhat absurd distortion, philosophy's response is to try to bring a measure of simple clarity to the caco-symphonic nature of human life. It works to accentuate the severe questionableness of human existence and understanding—always "the same" basic question, both exhilarating and terrifying, of being a thinking being and hence of being at all. It reflects on a grand scale the precarious hope of gathering together in the listening darkness and daring to make music around the glowing embers of history. Philosophy's contribution is orientation and reorientation to that rudimentary question of thinking and being, the original "fundament" of *Homo sapiens*. Trying to make the question explicit can have a profound, transformative effect on our everyday activities, just as laying down rhythm on the bodhrán can alter the penny whistle's character by adding the *gravitas* that is liable to be lost when played alone.

Understood like so, although philosophical theses attempt to "put everything before us" and so to strengthen our "deep common accord" by saying something fundamental about the preconditions of life as we live it, their contributions are resoundingly creative. Philosophy, like the drop of the down beat, does not stand in a world all by itself but acknowledges and anticipates and thereby sustains the total dynamic range of our questioning. Only because we can reflect on our accordance can we resolve our discord, and only because we partake in this prior accord can we consider its myriad potentials. We are simply becoming who we are when we harken to the general theme of world history, bringing ourselves before it explicitly here and now, that it be taken up again and again by our children.

I claim that education does all of this originally and without end. All educators everywhere, formal or otherwise, awaken their pupils to the primordial call of mind stretching back through forgotten epochs, and in time these children too will be teaching their own young—the new educators, sage elders, and blessed ancestors of the future. The task of philosophy is just to try to keep in view the basic achievements of thinking and being. At the heart of those always stand the achievements of education, because education is the original human achievement insofar as it introduces us, endlessly, to language and hence to reality, wherein thinking beings live and dwell. Education is the highest pursuit insofar as it opens the universe to us, by teaching us how to think for ourselves and for what we are. For its part, philosophy is just our returning to ourselves, to "the same"—to that original transformative achievement of education and so to the sheer happening of reality.

A Synopsis of the Chapters

These "philosophical theses" can seem merely to advance romantic but hollow metaphysical claims about education while nevertheless saying nothing useful about its actual practice. This is the concern, perhaps immediately recognizable, with which I begin Chapter 1. There I explain how philosophy has recently been undergoing a crisis of self-identity, where in the face of overwhelming demand for practical applicability—bolstered by the standing claim of fiscal duty—the discourse of philosophy of education has felt pressure to reduce itself to the role of conceptual underlaborer. That is alarming enough, but even more alarming is philosophy's doubting of its own capacities—even the latest and apparently the most modest one, the deadpan analysis of the concepts of language.

In response to this, I follow the thinking of Wittgenstein from his early days, where the very idea of concept analysis is just beginning to emerge, to his later philosophy, where language in its essential incompleteness admits of no final analysis. This latter insight, which is a way of seeing that "language takes care of itself" (Wittgenstein 1961: 43), sheds light on two broad approaches that now exist in educational philosophical discourse. Both approaches are laudable insofar as they try to maintain a practical maturity in the realm of theory by repudiating the rhetoric of foundationalism: philosophy cannot any longer, and did not really ever, stand on some higher level of analysis, dictating the conceptual or metaphysical foundations of the activities of people. Both approaches fail to appropriately recognize philosophy's enduring capacity, however, to continue to say things that are fundamental—though not foundational in the traditional sense—to the self-understanding of humans. Philosophy is about contemplating reality at large and making explicit the questions and worries we have about being in the world. This in turn reveals the fundamental connection that I believe holds between philosophy and education; for education too is concerned with coming to terms with reality insofar as, through it, young ones come to view themselves as individuals who live in the universe—whatever that may amount to.

In Chapter 2, I explore the idea that language is the medium of thought and the repository of historical mind, arguing that a child's acquisition of language is tantamount to her acquisition of rational freedom. Her education, broadly conceived, marks a metaphysical change: no longer merely an animal, she comes to exercise her powers of rationality, transcending her environment by seeking and expressing reasons for thinking and doing. She comes to be at home in the world, to be able to think about herself in relation to the universe, hence to philosophize and to educate others in turn.

I expand on the historical nature of language in Chapter 3, arguing that education locates us in uncompleted history, incompletely understood. Insofar as language is the repository of historical mind, the thinking already embedded in language always anticipates further questioning. I turn to etymology as a conceptual model for this kind of understanding: by studying the historical manifestation and development of words in light of their origins, etymology provides a general orientation toward, and understanding of, an incomplete conceptual whole. Philosophical understanding has this character too: that is why it can continue to yield fundamental insights. I demonstrate this possibility by attending to the etymologies of concepts like "education" and "understanding," construing education as a leading out into the midst of Being.

In Chapter 4, I bring the philosophical approach developed in previous chapters to bear on the very idea of an educational aim. I argue that discussion concerning the substantiality of educational ideals results in an impasse: one side insists on an open-ended understanding of education's aims, at the cost of seeming vague and impractical; the other insists on a more definitive account, at the cost of seeming small-minded and restrictive. I suggest educational ideals exhibit a conceptual duality: the fundamental achievements of education, such as rational freedom, are real; but how we should understand them, and how they might manifest themselves in an individual human life, remain open questions. It is therefore a standing task of educational philosophy to envision, enrich, and renew the aims of education according to the changing conditions of human life.

Chapter 5 is an attempt, first, to show that philosophical understanding is not extraneous to everyday human living. Philosophy is the fulfillment of rational freedom, and its insights have the creative capacity to effect large-scale transformation of our everyday activities—not least educational activities, such as the happenings of the classroom. Philosophy, conducted in historical, unfinished language, allows us to reach ever-new heights of understanding, so that we can return to the every day with new ways of understanding who and what we are. The fact that this transformative self-understanding is without end suggests further that the basic aims of education are *unheimlich*, deeply familiar and yet not at all. That is, our coming to be at home in the world through education is equally our coming to be not-at-home, because what it is to be a thinking being, and what a thinking being must ask of herself, are always open to question.

I conclude with speculative reflection on the shape and nature of language as an incomplete and self-governing whole, and with the *unheimlich* suggestion that, through education, reality awakens to itself.

Notes

1. Compare Richard J. Bernstein: "[Gadamer] wants to answer the question—to put it into Kantian terms—how is understanding possible?" (2008: 582) Cf. also Cavell: "[F]or Wittgenstein human language plays the role of the *a priori*. What we have 'always known' is the condition for our knowing anything whatever, namely human language" (2012b: 208).
2. The etymological remarks in this text are based mostly on *The Concise Oxford Dictionary of English Etymology* (1996), as well as on Robert K. Barnhart's (1988) *Dictionary of Etymology*, Carl Darling Buck's (1988) *A Dictionary of Selected Synonyms in the Principal Indo-European Languages*, Ernest Klein's (1971) *A Comprehensive Etymological Dictionary of the English Language*, and Ernest Weekley's (1967) *An Etymological Dictionary of Modern English*.

1

Education and Philosophy: A Crisis of Self-Identity

Between education and philosophy exists a fundamental conceptual connection whose nature, today, might be more difficult than ever to appreciate. Understood aright, education might become much more important, even central, to philosophy's conception of its own task; and education might come to recognize itself as a basically philosophical activity. As it stands, though, what is called the philosophy of education has to live with a kind of double outsider status: it is not recognized as a proper subdiscipline of philosophy, but it is not fully welcome in the formal educational establishment either.[1] This is astonishing, if only because our capacity for cultivating and communicating the wisdom of generations is a unique and essential feature of the human mode of being. In Kant's phrase, "Man is the only being who needs education" (1960: 1). After all, *Homo sapiens*—wise man—is what we call ourselves, philosophy itself having been named for our long-suffering pursuit of wisdom.

Before considering this connection, however, I first need to point out two main sources of opposition to it. These are significant because each represents, by turns from without and within the realm of explicit theory, a general form of skepticism about what philosophy can offer the educational enterprise. How philosophers of education react to such skepticism shapes their approach in a way that is liable to distort philosophy's broader self-image, further concealing the deeper unity between philosophy and education that I have in mind. Investigating these issues will allow me to address that connection in a more meaningful way, and the connection itself will turn out to be a central theme of the following chapters.

Can Philosophy Say Anything of Value to Education? Two Main Challenges

First, there is a challenge to philosophy's significance to education arising from outside the realm of explicit theoretical reflection. The idea is that philosophy is basically useless theory, whereas education is a key economic instrument. This popular way of thinking is supposedly grounded in the application of common sense to the fact of international economic integration, known colloquially as globalization, and crystallizing in what has been called the New Public Management, "new managerialism,"[2] or "corporate scientism" (Fairfield 2009: 25). It is a technical form of administration that applies instrumental reasoning to an ever-increasing demand for fiscal responsibility. Its principal aim is to maximize the economic performativity of educational institutions through efficient resource exploitation. It does this by emphasizing utility and quantification in order to standardize the transmission of knowledge and competencies while developing an increasingly competitive workforce. Knowledge and value are thereby reduced to economic units.[3]

It is implicit in this view that the aims of education are settled. Philosophy can say nothing substantial about it because educational institutions, policies, and practices are already subject to the ineluctable criteria of economic performativity, which are themselves in the sphere of statistical analysis and hence already within the orbit of scientific methodology. As Michael Peters and Kenneth Wain put it, "National education systems in the contemporary era are still caught between satisfying these twin demands: the administrative reason of the state apparatus and the technical reason promoted by the market and industrialization in general" (2003: 58). Theoretical reflection, on the other hand, is regarded with impatience given the conventional demand for determinate output. Educational research is encouraged not at the level of open theory familiar to philosophers but in forms specifically geared to influence policy that is economically motivated and articulated in economic terms.

This may seem an obnoxious caricature of the attitude in question, and not actually reflective of current affairs in education; but it is the prevailing official view and has been for decades on a global scale. Consider the language of the following four reports on national and international educational aims and policy by governmentally appointed bodies in North America and Europe: the 1983 US National Commission on Excellence in Education, the 1997 British National Committee of Inquiry into Higher Education, the

2001 Education Council to the Council of Europe, and the 2012 Advisory Panel on Canada's International Education Strategy. The central theme of these reports is, without a doubt, international competitiveness in a knowledge-based economy. There is often the bonus disclaimer that the humanistic and cultural values cultivated by education should not be given purely economic significance, but in each case the motivating idea is that education is above all an internationally strategic economic instrument. Here are some excerpts:

> Our Nation is at risk. Our once unchallenged preeminence in commerce, industry, science, and technological innovation is being overtaken by competitors throughout the world. ... We have, in effect, been committing an act of unthinking, unilateral educational disarmament.
>
> Our society and its educational institutions seem to have lost sight of the basic purposes of schooling ... Knowledge, learning, information, and skilled intelligence are the new raw materials of international commerce and are today spreading throughout the world ... Learning is the indispensable investment required for success in the "information age" we are entering. Our concern, however, goes well beyond matters such as industry and commerce. It also includes the intellectual, moral, and spiritual strengths of our people which knit together the very fabric of our society. The people of the United States need to know that individuals in our society who do not possess the levels of skill, literacy, and training essential to this new era will be effectively disenfranchised, not simply from the material rewards that accompany competent performance, but also from the chance to participate fully in our national life.
>
> (United States 1983)

> In doing so [i.e., in observing "the changing context for higher education" in the UK], we do not accept a purely instrumental approach to higher education. Its distinctive character must lie in the independent pursuit of knowledge and understanding. But higher education has become central to the economic wellbeing of nations and individuals. The qualities of mind that it develops will be the qualities that society increasingly needs to function effectively. Knowledge is advancing so rapidly that a modern competitive economy depends on its ability to generate that knowledge, engage with it and use it to effect.
>
> (United Kingdom 1997: 51)

> On the basis of contributions from Member States the Council has identified a number of common priorities for the future and the contribution which the education and training systems must make if the Lisbon goal that Europe should become "*the most competitive and dynamic knowledge-based economy in*

the world, capable of sustainable economic growth with more and better jobs and greater social cohesion" is to be achieved. At the same time, the Council notes the principle that an important role of Education is to promote the humanistic values shared by our societies.

(Council of Europe 2001; original italics)

Our vision for Canada: become the 21st century leader in international education in order to attract top talent and prepare our citizens for the global marketplace, thereby providing key building blocks for our future prosperity. ... The panel is committed to the concept that the international education strategy should uphold and illuminate Canada's brand of quality and excellence. Additionally, we are of the opinion that such a strategy will align with other important national strategies (such as Canada's S & T strategy, a revamped immigration strategy and a labour market strategy) and complement existing and future comprehensive economic and trade agreements. ... The panel believes that Canada has a competitive advantage over many other countries, including Australia, New Zealand, the United States and the United Kingdom. The time to act is now so that Canada's full potential in international education can be fully realized.

(Canada 2012: viii, ix–x)

It cannot be denied that there is acknowledgment here of educational aims and values that are non-instrumental, but it is already beside the point to argue that those should be pursued for their own sake, as ends in themselves, whatever the other objectives of education. Recognizing the promotion of "the independent pursuit of knowledge and understanding" and of "the humanistic values shared by our societies" as "an important role" of education is really subordinate to the underlying theme of international economic competitiveness. It is an aside. It can then only be an artificial consolation to theorize about the "intrinsic value" of education, since any description of educational values that does not coincide with an instrumental description is effectively meaningless according to the criteria of economic performativity.[4] In fact those "qualities of mind" said to be developed by higher education are, for the British National Committee above, meaningful precisely insofar as they help society "function effectively," to "generate ... knowledge, engage it and use it to effect" in pursuit of a "modern competitive economy." For the European Education Council, educated "social cohesion" is directly associated with a "competitive and dynamic knowledge-based economy." For Canada's Advisory Panel, "quality and excellence" in education is considered a national "brand" to be marketed worldwide, together with "other important national strategies" for economic leadership. For the US National Commission, the "intellectual, moral, and spiritual strengths of our people" are necessary for citizens "to participate fully in our national life"—the life, however, of a "[n]ation at risk" of self-imposed "educational disarmament" and the loss of an internationally "unchallenged preeminence." These are, again, instrumental valuations of education that have long been the norm and remain so today.[5]

According to the new managerialism, theoretical reflection about the nature and aims of education is empty if it does not obey "the imperative to demonstrate impact" (Standish 2011: x), an ultimately economic imperative that extends to academia generally and to the philosophy of education in particular. The imperative is implicit, however, because pervasive: it has become "plain common sense." The default data-driven analysis and economic parlance of such reports as the above are for the sake of their official readers, those making important political and financial decisions, not for those interested in actually thinking about what education is. For the new managerialism, to think about education is not to ask what it is, but what it is for; and that is hardly a "philosophical" question.

The other main challenge to philosophy's significance to education comes from within the realm of theory proper, but it can bear a practical resemblance to the above view. The objection here is that, according to the insights of postmodern or late analytic forms of thought, philosophy has deprived itself of the right to pronounce on the varieties of human inquiry. Philosophy, it is argued, has canceled its own traditional authority to lecture on the metaphysical or conceptual foundations of intellectual activities, because there is no longer any reason to believe in the reality of, or in the need for, such foundations.

This antifoundationalist attitude can lead to a generalized skepticism about what philosophy can contribute to education. At the unlikely extreme, it might culminate in a subjectivist or relativist[6] denial of real educational values, so that deeper reflection on the nature and aims of education becomes redundant or impossible. A perceived task might then be to deconstruct without reconstructing the inherited ideals and ideologies dominating the education system. This may include trying to destroy outright all forms of politics, power, and institutional and curricular structure, along with any accepted canons of educational theory. That purely nihilistic approach, however, is not properly attributable to any contemporary philosopher of education, even though the idea behind it is not one to be ignored.[7]

Under a less aggressive skepticism, the actual practice of education might enjoy renewed emphasis, since it can appear not to require philosophical support, being able to get along just as well on its own. Learning, after all, can occur in spite of teaching, and teaching in spite of theorizing about it.[8] Many educators in the public system, myself included, resist the often condescending, top-down emphasis on "professional development" that is in vogue today.[9] Education is, often enough, something that just happens; so the suspicion is that philosophical abstraction only serves to distract from real-life concerns. The philosophy of education can then seem applicable only as a branch of practical or applied philosophy, where its humble task is to hone the analytical tools of policymaking and curriculum design.

Put like that, it is easy to see how a working alliance can form between antifoundationalism and the new managerialism, in light of which philosophizing about education looks entirely parasitic. This complementarity, added to the enduring modern vision of philosophy as conceptual underlaborer to natural science, helps explain why educational research takes place far more in the institutes and professional schools of education than in philosophy departments. Mistrust of philosophical reflection remains widespread and presents a real obstacle to an authentic philosophy of education.[10]

Education's Need for Genuine Philosophical Reflection

Anyone who believes that the educational endeavor does stand in need of genuine philosophical reflection must confront the two challenges outlined above. They might reject the first—the new managerialism, which behaves as though it is beyond theory—by identifying the normative assumptions implicit in granting instrumental reasoning the status of common sense; they might also try to generate skepticism about how sensible, or even how common, common sense really is. The idea here is that one cannot elude theoretical assumptions or the possibility of their being criticized, and this is particularly true of education, an ancient activity whose history is rich with theoretical and practical diversity. The new managerialism—its economic imperatives obeyed by governments, educational committees, and administrators alike—itself constitutes a philosophical approach to education. The approach is to sentence education to the sphere of economic performativity at the expense of other values that are highly significant, even essential, to human living. As such it is not above criticism, even though it gives the impression of absolute inevitability.

This objection, however, while clearly appropriate, is perhaps already too abstract for those who are practically involved with formal or public education in a professional capacity—who feel that there is something deeply wrong with it, but who cannot easily express their anxieties. The default imperative for economic responsibility may seem a kind of *jus primae noctis*, but it can be difficult to say exactly what the problem is, since the imperative's instrumental logic is so difficult to think beyond. Besides, as I noted above, policy documents often leave explicit room for theorizing about educational aims and values as ends in themselves, a patronizing consolation that at the same time undermines the very framework in which such talk makes sense.

Instead, what is most disturbing about the new managerialism may emerge as an almost instinctual awareness that under it the virtue of education is being jeopardized, and needs insulating from the atmosphere of constant economic crisis and national risk that is integral to the success of "such growth industries as school effectiveness and school improvement" (Blake et al. 2003: 13). It may come to light, in other words, that the practical integrity of education, however allergic to abstractionism, now needs genuine theoretical protection—and that this need has begun to ripen under the Orwellian glow cast by the new managerialism.

How philosophers face the second challenge, though—that philosophy has given up its right to pronounce, from the realm of high theory, on whatever enterprise it beholds—is more complicated than the almost visceral reaction to the new managerialism just mentioned. The problem is not just that the possibility for reflective thinking is being blocked systemically by a ubiquitous economic imperative. More than that, reflective thinking has come to doubt its own efficacy. For the philosophy of education, this amounts to a self-conscious anxiety about its own basic situation. Because the anxiety is founded on genuine insights, however, which connect up with more global philosophical issues, it is difficult to do away with neatly.[11]

It is therefore necessary to understand the force of those insights that gave rise to antifoundationalism and to the ensuing skepticism about philosophy's significance to education. I have already mentioned that the actual practice of education seems to get along on its own without the kind of theorizing philosophers often think it needs. Ludwig Wittgenstein is famous for his analogous insights about language, another distinctive human activity; and because those insights have been fundamental to the development of antifoundationalism, it is important to understand Wittgenstein's thinking here.

To focus on language will be instructive for at least three reasons. The first is the one just cited: both education and language are distinctly human activities,[12] and yet both exhibit a practical integrity that does not automatically require theoretical support. Seeing how language resists traditional philosophical attempts to "ground" it will help shed light on the analogous skepticism about sincere philosophical treatments of education. Second, language has been a principal focus of general philosophy for more than a century: questions about the nature of language and its relationship to thought have played a major role in philosophy's understanding of itself. This, third, will help elucidate some of the approaches to education that philosophers nevertheless see available in light of the emerging antifoundationalism. Their reactions approximate those of other philosophers, such as Richard Rorty, who are alive to the broader issue about the place of philosophy in human discourse—those who want to take seriously the insight about the practical integrity of education and language, but who still think deeper reflection about the human condition is possible and worthwhile.

A final way in which the focus on language will be appropriate is this: it will introduce the fundamental connection that I think holds between philosophy and education, one yet deeper than is normally acknowledged.

Wittgenstein on Language

Wittgenstein's guiding insight was twofold: first, language is more intimately connected to thought than we typically allow; second, philosophy abuses language by attempting to think through to the foundations of knowledge and discourse in order to "ground" them "philosophically." In short, language can take care of itself. The most famous expression, however misguided, of this dual insight is found at the end of the first and only work Wittgenstein published in his lifetime—the *Tractatus Logico-Philosophicus*—where he portrays the very propositions that comprise that work as betraying its own basic thought: that we must pass in silence over that of which we cannot speak (2007: §§6.54–7).[13] Even before this, however, Wittgenstein means to "recognize *how* language takes care of itself" (1961: 43), and part of his lasting appeal is that he is never quite settled on how to properly situate this insight.[14]

His early, logico-mystical thinking is this. Although the tautological propositions of logic "mirror"[15] the metaphysical trinity of world, language, and thought,[16] language cannot meaningfully describe itself;[17] so any such propositions, strictly speaking, "say nothing."[18] This leads Wittgenstein to say in his "Lecture on Ethics," for example, "that the right expression in language for the miracle of the existence of the world, though it is not any proposition *in* language, is the existence of language itself" (1929: 44; original italics). Language, hence thought, is limited insofar as it cannot make its own form explicit. It would be nonsensical, for instance, to try to describe the metaphysical subject—the "I," the speaker of propositions, of language—because it is not in the world but constitutes a logical boundary of the world.[19] Language takes care of itself by reflecting its form and limits in every meaningful expression, but language is meaningful only within those limits, where it states facts clearly. For the early Wittgenstein, recognizing the limits of language would ensure the meaningfulness of discourse through a steadfast silence with respect to ethics, aesthetics, and metaphysics: like logic, they state no facts (2007: §§6.41–6.421, 6.53). With the limits of meaningful expression in place, the course could be set for the systematic clarification of language, hence of thought, and for their twin commitment to natural science, whose task is to determine empirically all that is the case.[20]

There is a serious tension, however, in any attempt to draw a clear limit "to the expression of thoughts" (Wittgenstein 2007: 3), or to meaningful language in general. Meaning seems to crop up everywhere, often precisely where there is meant to be none. It is a tension that the *Tractatus*'s declarations about its own meaninglessness could not quite transcend, but to which Wittgenstein devoted much of his later thinking. The project of the *Tractatus* was like that of a cartographer journeying to the ends of the earth to mark them off once and for all. Wittgenstein ended where he began—with the insight that language somehow takes care of itself, but unable to articulate it in a way that was both clear and sufficiently profound. Yet it was not just that Wittgenstein unapologetically embraced a metaphysical picture of language while declaring metaphysics nonsense.[21] The deeper problem was that his picture distorted language itself.

In the *Philosophical Investigations*, a later work published only posthumously, Wittgenstein admits feeling "forced to recognize grave mistakes" in the *Tractatus* (1958: viii), signaling his return to the practical integrity of language with renewed suspicion of philosophical theorizing. In his early thinking he had glimpsed the importance of attending to the actual usage of words and propositions in natural speech,[22] but at the time this had meant "all the propositions of our everyday language, just as they stand, are in perfect logical order" (2007: §5.5563), and by bringing out this order we could make perspicuous what can and cannot be said or thought. Even in what is sometimes called the middle period of his thinking, Wittgenstein declares himself "interested in language as a procedure according to explicit rules," which if properly defined would reveal philosophy's traditional problems to be purely linguistic misunderstandings (1974: 68). A little later, however, he begins to view these rules and their related concepts—including the concept "proposition"—as exhibiting only a family resemblance, having "no sharp boundary" with respect either to the practices upon which they are founded or to their meaningful application (1958: §54; 1972: §§318–21). He also gives up the related belief that language can be analyzed down to its "elementary propositions" (2007: §5.5562) and objects of reference.[23] With that, he gives up the greater goal of totalizing clarity[24]—of bringing language to a "state of complete exactness" (1958: §91) or "crystalline purity" (§108)—a "single completely resolved form of every expression" (§91):

> When I say: "My broom is in the corner,"—is this really a statement about a broomstick and the brush? Well, it could at any rate be replaced by a statement giving the position of the stick and the position of the brush. ... Then does someone who says that the broom is in the corner really mean: the broomstick is there, and so is the brush, and the broomstick is fixed in the brush?—If we were to ask anyone if he meant this he would probably say that he had not thought specially of the broomstick or specially of the brush at all. And that would be the *right* answer, for he meant to speak neither of the stick nor of the brush in particular.
>
> (§60; original italics)

Here Wittgenstein demonstrates the absurdity of the idea that conceptual analysis reveals what we "really mean" when we say something, as though a sentence "has one and only one complete analysis" (2007: §3.25). It also illustrates the renewed prominence Wittgenstein places on everyday language as a self-regulating activity. While it is possible to say more about the broomstick and the brush, that does not mean the original, unanalyzed statement is somehow lacking: it does not require analysis at all; analysis in this case distorts the statement's original intent.[25] This leads to his mature view of language as fundamentally incomplete, responding in continuous self-formation to the shifting practical realities of life.[26] Wittgenstein even goes on to describe the "world-picture" of language as just "the inherited background against which I distinguish between true and false"—"a kind of mythology," a "river-bed of thoughts" liable to "shift" according to the currents of history (1972: §§94–9).

For the later Wittgenstein, language takes care of itself in a way that philosophy cannot supersede, by inverting the very idea of a need for conceptual foundations: "I have arrived at the rock bottom of my convictions. And one might almost say that these foundation-walls are carried by the whole house" (2007: §248). Philosophical attempts at laying the groundwork for the integrity of language in the service of scientific clarity were themselves assaults on that integrity: such was the failure of the *Tractatus*. Wittgenstein's enduring suggestion was for philosophical investigation to become self-consciously therapeutic, "a battle against the bewitchment of our intelligence by means of language" (1958: §109).

Any aid that philosophy could offer the integrity of language would be to protect it from philosophy's own confusions, not to construct an indestructible theory that would "ground" it once and for all.

Educational Philosophy after Wittgenstein

What does this mean for education? Wittgenstein's attempts to articulate his insight about language highlight philosophy's tendency to act as a theoretical parasite, breeding confusion where there need be none; and his reconceptualization of philosophy as its own antidote has resonated across the disciplines. Although Wittgenstein was by no means alone in his criticisms of traditional philosophy, his thinking has contributed significantly to the twentieth-century rise of antifoundationalism, the belief that philosophy can no longer conceive of itself as providing the foundations for other human activities, including education: "Explanations must come to an end somewhere" (1958: §1; cf. 1972: §§164, 192).

Richard Rorty has been a prominent critic of philosophy in a similar manner, and his view of the consequences of philosophy's turn to language owes much to the later Wittgenstein. One such consequence is that philosophical problems do not constitute a "natural kind" (2007c: 165) but are products of intellectual "doxography"—of attempts either to universalize a problematic based on a supposedly foundational canon of literature, or to found a literary canon based on a supposedly universal problematic (1984: 261).[27] Down at "the nitty-gritty of intellectual history," however, "the distinctions between great and non-great dead philosophers, between clear and borderline cases of 'philosophy', and between philosophy, literature, politics, religion, and social science are of less and less importance" (1984: 269). Since philosophy's hope of crystallizing the foundations of knowledge and discourse came up empty, Rorty suggests it dissolve itself into the rest of academia, forming a kind of historically enlightened cultural politics—a seamless discipline that would absorb philosophy's residues as intellectuals turn from foundational questions to more tangible ones (1983: 76). For Rorty, the history of discourse is a tapestry of vocabularies and language practices woven by expediency (cf. 1989c); what we need now is to "reweave" and recontextualize in order to help manage today's practical issues (1989b: 85).

Rorty says little about education as such, and does not think philosophy should either (1990: 41), but many philosophers of education have taken his more general view to heart. Even if they cannot exactly allow philosophy's closing up shop, the idea that theoretical work now demands a variety of perspectives, each roughly on a par with one another and emphasizing practical outcomes, is popular. I quote the editors of the *Blackwell Guide to the Philosophy of Education*:

> What [philosophy] can no longer do … is stand itself on a different level of analysis, and hence of authority, prescribing and proscribing *de haut en bas*—a stance in which the underlaborer suddenly turns out to be a king in disguise. Other disciplines have, in recent decades, sharpened their own higher-level understanding of their own projects. They expect to speak to philosophers at the same level of abstraction (if they speak to them at all), and often by reference to the same literatures. Furthermore, at least some schools of philosophy have achieved a greater self-consciousness about the extraphilosophical pressures that constrain and mold their own practices. Perhaps most significantly of all, the conception of philosophy as sovereign can only rest on precisely that faith in foundations which, as we have seen, is now generally lost. Arguably, debate between philosophy and other disciplines needs now to be an engagement on equal terms and with less concern for territory.
>
> (Blake et al. 2003: 15)[28]

Let us bring into view the main historical target of this polemic in the philosophy of education. The image of the underlaborer-turned-king is, for the most part, supposed to represent what has been called the London School led by R. S. Peters, Robert Dearden, and Paul Hirst.[29] These philosophers, whose heyday was in the 1960s and 1970s, encouraged submitting all forms of educational discourse, including scientific approaches, to conceptual analysis. Like the early Wittgenstein, they believed "metaphysics and epistemology" as a philosophical problematic could be ignored in favor of the logical clarification of concepts, and so they anticipated setting the educational endeavor on a firm conceptual foundation. The result would be a justifiable confidence in the rational nature of the curriculum and ultimately of what was being taught in schools. They too were critical of tradition and, like the young Wittgenstein, believed that careful attention to the logic of language would lead to a kind of totalizing clarity. Hirst's expression in *Knowledge and the Curriculum* is illustrative:

> Philosophy … is above all concerned with the clarification of the concepts and propositions through which our experience and activities are intelligible … [I]t is not a speculative super-science that tries to answer questions about some ultimate reality; it is not the pursuit of moral knowledge; it is not the great integrator of all human understanding into a unified view of man, God and the Universe; it is not a science—as is, for instance, psychology or sociology—concerned to understand what is the case in terms of experiment and observation. It is

rather a distinctive pursuit, primarily an analytical pursuit, with the ambition of understanding the concepts used in all other forms of lower-order knowledge and awareness ... concerned above all with the necessary features of our primary forms of understanding and awareness in the sciences, in morals, in history and the like.

(1975: 1)[30]

The London School's approach was explicitly modest in comparison to the heady aspirations of traditional philosophy. It was not a metaphysical undertaking, but a conceptual one that would clarify the language of other modes of discourse in the service of education. This professed modesty underpinned the popular image of the conceptual underlaborer.[31]

As modesty, however, if not exactly false, it was perhaps misplaced. Although the idea of philosophy as the "great integrator of human knowledge" faced explicit rejection, it survived with the goal of "understanding the concepts used in all other forms of lower-order knowledge and awareness." Moreover, central to the approach was the idea that clear limits to the meaning and application of concepts could really be drawn, perhaps once and for all.[32] As with Wittgenstein's experience with language, though, this "prescriptive and proscriptive" agenda would do further violence to the integrity of educational discourse by attempting to force the relevant language into fixed schemes of meaning and application, and to control curriculum design. Hirst himself eventually admits that "the spell of the analytical techniques" and "the spell of a hard rationalism," both characteristic of British philosophy of education in the 1960s and 1970s, "have been broken" (1993: 184), so that "education can no longer be rationalistically planned" (194). The idea of a "spell" that had been "cast" recalls the later Wittgenstein's imperative to resist "the bewitchment of our intelligence by means of language." For the London School, this had been to imagine itself enumerating the conceptual foundations of education and of a rationally justifiable curriculum: "The main error in my position," writes Hirst, "was seeing theoretical knowledge as the logical foundation for the development of sound practical knowledge and rational personal development" (197). Yet rather than arguing for the inverse, for the logical "priority of practical knowledge in education" over theoretical knowledge, he now sees this practical domain as a "complex of specific, substantive social practices with all the knowledge, attitudes, feelings, virtues, skills, dispositions and relationships that that involves" (197). The complex, as such, resists final analysis.

David Carr sums up the widespread transition in educational philosophy from conceptual analysis to a discourse without foundations:

> While the utility of epistemological reflection for curriculum studies and even for practical curriculum development should not be dismissed entirely ... it is clear that the new analytical educational philosophy considerably overestimated its scope and potential in crediting it with a foundational role in curriculum planning. What epistemologists of recent times have generally come to see is ... knowledge is inherently provisional, and ... we are not entitled to regard any of our current theories, explanations and truth claims as beyond the possibility of revision in the light of new evidence of one sort or another. ...
>
> Thus, not only is the ship of human knowledge unavailable for complete rational reconstruction at sea, it is also sailing in uncharted waters and is liable for repair at any given moment due to damage from reefs unseen. Hence, the foundationalist epistemology of the Enlightenment gives way to a contemporary or "postmodern" epistemology of discourse in which nothing is fixed and final and all questions of epistemological value are, in principle, open.
>
> (1999: 178–9)

If philosophy can no longer lay claim to a foundationalist approach, however, and if in the end "nothing is fixed," what is the philosophy of education supposed to accomplish?

I claimed above that philosophers of education react in a more complicated way to the challenge of antifoundationalism than to the new managerialism. Now it is easier to see why. Those who believe that education would benefit from theoretical treatment, but who also acknowledge that philosophy has given up its traditional claim to foundational thinking, must reconcile these two insights. They believe deeper reflection on the nature and aims of education is neither impossible nor empty, but urgent in light of the new managerialism; but they also want to respect education's integrity. They want to take antifoundationalism seriously, but in a way that still allows for effective debate about education, because such theoretical reflection has become of practical importance.

Two Approaches to Educational Philosophy: Therapy and Cultural Politics

From here, two broad ways in which philosophy can contribute authentically to the educational endeavor become visible.[33] The first derives from Wittgenstein's idea of philosophy as therapy, and it is based on the idea of bewitchment by language. Although renewed attention to language is an undeniable critical asset, however, a preference for exactitude is not the mark of this approach.

What is needed is a practical maturity in theoretical discussion, wrought from the painful temptation to utter what Wittgenstein calls "that inarticulate sound with which many writers would like to begin philosophy" (1975: §68). Philosophers possess this experiential advantage and can point out areas of educational debate and policy that are ineffective because based on confused assumptions. The hope is to show how those assumptions have done violence to education's integrity, to its ordinary nature and aims. In that sense, philosophical therapy animates the true spirit of analytic philosophy insofar as it removes obstructions to our normal understanding.[34] Philosophers can seek restitution by working to unravel the conceptual knots that they and their predecessors had been caught in, but much of this involves convincing the interested parties that the threads need to stay loosened or even that they require loosening in the first place.[35]

An obvious target for such therapy is the new managerialism. Statements that appear scientifically informed feature prominently in the language of educational administration. One example is the characterization of competence. Often this consists of "identikit" words, phrases, and sentences—tools for constructing profiles that represent exactitude and thoroughness, and advertise efficiency by facilitating classification and rank. Here is one criticism of this routine practice:

> The idea of the profile is in part to provide a more accurate account of the pupil's experience and attainment on the course. It also fits in with the principle of recording positive achievement. Arguably it will be more meaningful to employers and parents than a numerical mark or grade. But it is clear that the language of the profile is doomed to be mechanistic so long as it is drawn from a list of stock phrases. There is perhaps something disingenuous about the presentation of an extended and seemingly thorough report on a student when this has in fact been produced in this way.
>
> (Standish 1992: 260)

That is of course not the end of the matter. In the first place, producing the kind of personalized profile demanded by critics of the new managerialism would require greater proximity between instructor and pupil, further exhausting classroom resources; plus, the instructor's assessment efforts will have to intensify dramatically if stock phrases are disallowed, and worse, a pupil's competence will become hostage to the instructor's ability to articulate it; finally, from an employer's perspective, standardizing language facilitates ease of comparison, reinforcing the expediency required of any capable organization.

Such a reply clearly depends on assumptions about the demands of resource efficiency, however. It is not just that this view unquestioningly assumes the inevitability of such demands. It assumes this in a way that diverts attention from its presupposing positive facts about competence, which the assessment is expected to communicate accurately in a bid to influence the proper allocation and transaction of resources. This assumption downplays the real contact of human beings that forms the background of the possibility of such "facts" and whose personal meaningfulness ultimately pervades every such "resource transaction." As Raymond Callahan writes as early as 1962 in *Education and the Cult of Efficiency*,

> It was not that some of the ideas from the business world might not have been used to advantage in educational administration, but that the wholesale adoption of the basic values, as well as the techniques of the business-industrial world, was a serious mistake in an institution whose primary purpose was the education of children.
>
> (244)

A debate about assessment practices that ignores the human in educational interaction is simply misguided.

A second, more constructive approach in the philosophy of education multiplies theoretical perspectives based on the vast literary, artistic, scientific, and cultural histories that constitute our intellectual inheritance. This is in harmony with Richard Rorty's suggestion of a cultural politics, an interweaving of texts with a view to shedding light on matters of practical and theoretical currency. Randall Curren argues that

> much of what is most admirable in philosophy of education pertains to the politics and ethics of education … [T]he wealth of recent work on the history of philosophy … has been salutary in documenting the wealth of attention to educational questions through much of the history of philosophy, and in retrieving forgotten but valuable ways of thinking about education.
>
> (2008: 1)

To the politics and ethics of education, philosophy not only offers plenty of experience with the complexities of theorizing, as does the therapeutic approach; it also contributes a vast literature containing many perspectives on education.[36] The broad aim is to promote open and honest debate throughout different areas of educational theory and research, and the image of multiplying vocabularies, metaphors, and theoretical frameworks is meant to illustrate this.

I should stress, however, that such activity is not appropriately described as the indiscriminate application of readymade theoretical frameworks to practical educational matters: a more suitable characterization of the approach would be what Claudia Ruitenberg calls "discursive translation" (2010a: 112). Whereas the idea of applying a theory "suggests a unidirectional move," every act of translation involves a confrontation with "untranslatability," which is itself valuably productive for theorizing (113). Related to this is the innovative effect of a "deliberately committed ... discursive impertinence"—the deliberate and salutary recontextualization, or "displacement," of a theory, text, or idea in the search for new insight (112). Given the constructive, provisional nature of the translational approach, the expectation of arriving at some ideal theory or practical state of affairs is, or should be, conspicuously absent, but so too the likelihood of an impasse. The atmosphere is meant not so much to be one of intellectual conflict as of hospitality, not because of a lack of authentic critical engagement, but because of the lack of belief in a single and inflexible way of putting things, backed by the sober awareness of responding to genuine practical and theoretical problems in education. The "accomplishments" of educational theory on this approach are not foundational accomplishments but the birth of insight and the realization of piecemeal change on the ground level.[37]

Therapy and cultural politics are two general ways of continuing to engage in educational philosophical reflection in light of antifoundationalism, and they both enjoy popularity today. Not everyone would identify closely with either approach, but much of what is valuable in contemporary discussion will, arguably, take the shape of one or the other.[38] At any rate there appears a general consensus that issues in educational theory and practice call for, and philosophical work exhibits, a variety of styles and approaches:

> Sometimes complex philosophical enquiry is needed to expose and unravel the conceptual knots in which the discourse of educational theory and practice has become caught up. Sometimes the approach to questions of value requires a changing of the prevailing discourse in ways that fly in the face of common and professional understanding, precisely because it has become steeped in that discourse. Sometimes there are lines of thought developed by major philosophers, ancient and modern, that are worthy of exploration and interpretation, where attempts at simple exegesis can only end in a travesty of such views. Sometimes it is desirable to take risks in what is thought and said.
> (Blake et al. 2000: 16)

It is not difficult to see how my characterization of two broad approaches—roughly negative and roughly positive, or therapeutic and constructive—to the philosophy of education aligns with the above. Ideally, both approaches emphasize respect for the practical integrity of their subject matter, as also for other theoretical frameworks and other modes and methods of discourse. Both involve the practice of interpretation insofar as philosophers try to engage a topic with "careful attention and intention" (Ruitenberg 2010a: 112), with a degree of openness to complexity, ambiguity, and new ways of thinking, and with the kind of maturity, characteristic of the later Wittgenstein, that allows them to know when to stop pressing the issue in a certain direction. This maturity, though, comes from a special kind of experience.

The Scope of Language

There may remain doubts about whether these two ways of reflecting philosophically about education can honestly respect its practical integrity. After all, Wittgenstein's insight was that language can take care of itself, and philosophy must show appropriate restraint; and we have seen analogous unease between philosophy and education. Should not philosophy, having alienated itself from the ground level of human life, now never "interfere," but in its rehabilitated form investigate only in a way that "leaves everything as it is" (1958: §124)? Does not referring to philosophical reflection as an interpretive practice, as though it could relate to and have real effects on its subject matter, ignore the very distinction that would facilitate its modest return?

To object in this way would, I think, just be to reiterate the antifoundationalist challenge while misconstruing Wittgenstein's insight, even if Wittgenstein himself was never quite settled on how to situate it; or, if he was, perhaps it is we who should not feel so settled.[39] It is important to remember that while language takes care of itself, philosophy still happens in language. When we engage in philosophy, we still move within that broader domain of meaningfulness, of general human interaction, that forms the background of our questioning. We are indeed liable, in Wittgenstein's unfortunate phrase, to act "like savages, primitive people, who hear the expressions of civilized men, put a false interpretation on them, and then draw the queerest conclusions from it" (1958: §194). Yet we can, as Wittgenstein did, come to recognize our errors; but then how can we do this? Hans-Georg Gadamer's answer is splendid: "Is it not, in fact, the case that every misunderstanding presupposes a 'deep common accord' (1966b: 7)?"[40] The bewitchments of philosophy are recognizable only because in its greatest abstractions it still presupposes some deep commonality with natural language, with ordinary human being—just as every language, dialect, and jargon presupposes some deep commonality with every other. There are no savages.

To insist, therefore, that philosophical theorizing about linguistic practices is necessarily alien to such practice is to underestimate the scope of language. The *Tractatus* was meant to be a kind of ladder that the reader would throw away after transcending the nonsensicality of its propositions and coming to see the world aright (2007: §6.54). That is to recommend a clear boundary between what can and cannot be said, what can and cannot be thought; but the very idea of our being able to climb the ladder and then throw it away makes it questionable whether we can imagine that boundary. Wittgenstein's greatest bewitchment was to conclude, "What we cannot speak of we must pass over in silence" (2007: §7). That is in part why he returned to philosophy with a new openness to the complexity of the dimensions of language. To realize that language can take care of itself is to realize that any misunderstanding is already part of the deeper linguistic practices forming the "riverbed" of our thoughts. Language takes care of itself not through silence, but through the continued renewal of discourse. We should try to be aware of our misunderstandings, prejudices, confusions, questions, and contradictions, not out of disgust or a naïve desire to be rid of them once and for all, but because they of all things can point the way to a better understanding of the world.

It does not matter here whether we say that philosophical reflection is a special kind of linguistic practice, or is implicated in all sorts of practice, or that it arises naturally out of practice, or that there is a continuous play between them, into which all of us are always already thrown.[41] The point is reflection about language is close to language because it happens in language.[42] That is why it is so difficult to do,[43] but so we should also recognize its great importance. If philosophy can pay attention to this closeness, and try to see its activities as interpretive activities, mature and open, sometimes creative and sometimes not, without imagining that it must think through to the metaphysical or conceptual foundations of things, then perhaps it can exist somewhere between empty verbosity and hopeless silence.

Conclusion

I have not yet said anything about a fundamental connection between philosophy and education, to which I alluded at the start of this chapter. Instead I have attempted to clarify how philosophy can reflect about education while acknowledging Wittgenstein's insight that philosophy cannot take itself to be laying the foundations for human discourse. The way I expressed the insight, following Wittgenstein, was by saying that language takes care of itself. Acknowledging the insight was necessary, because to speak of philosophy as enjoying a fundamental connection with education sounds very much like trying to lay the foundations for a grand theory of education; and that is not something I want to do. From the last section, however, it may seem that the connection I hope to recognize is just that between theory as such and practice as such; but to leave it there might distort philosophy's self-image by making it seem like philosophy is just one interpretive perspective among others, and is therefore still at some conceptual remove from the educational endeavor. This, though, would conceal the deeper relation between the two, and I believe it is a shortcoming of much contemporary educational philosophy that the connection remains so concealed.[44]

To see through this, consider Rorty's suggestion that, in light of antifoundationalism, philosophy should simply dissolve itself into the other disciplines. Now if it is possible to imagine philosophy doing this—spreading itself out more or less evenly among the many strains of inquiry—it means philosophy is exceptional and not really at all on a par with those other disciplines. As I have been insisting, however, that does not mean philosophy is somehow sovereign. Rather, if we can agree that other disciplines have, to repeat an earlier phrase, "sharpened their own higher-level understanding of their own projects" (Blake et al. 2003: 15), I think the higher-level understanding of which those disciplines are partaking is not some higher-level understanding of which philosophy might also partake. It is philosophy itself, and to think otherwise would be to miss something deep about what philosophy is.

Rorty comes close to this view when he quotes Wilfrid Sellars's famous remark about philosophy, that it is "an attempt to see how things, in the broadest possible sense of the term, hang together, in the broadest possible sense of the term" (e.g., 1982: xiv; cf. Sellars 1963b: 1); but for Rorty that means because philosophy "shades off" into the other disciplines,[45] and because it can no longer conceive of itself as grounding anything, it has no special mandate. Philosophy does have a special mandate, however, insofar as it is uniquely explicit about the unlimitedness of what it is willing to look into. Philosophy is not unique in that it has a special territory, which it must mark out and defend; it is unique in that it disregards territory altogether because it is interested in reality at large.[46]

This helps disclose the fundamental connection that holds between philosophy and education. Education too does not, cannot have any regard for territory, because it must conceive of something to say to this curious and eager new generation of human beings—and the next, and every future generation—

already waking, stirring in the shadows, harkening to and taking up the steady call of the universe. All of history's educators, speaking for the children's sake, speak also for us, their living ancestors. Philosophy and education then must always dwell on the same crisis: the crisis of self-identity, of self-understanding as such. It is everyone's crisis, and it is what leads people to study philosophy in the first place. Wittgenstein sometimes imagined that the real discovery in philosophy is that which allows us to stop doing it—the one that "gives philosophy peace, so that it is no longer tormented by questions which bring *itself* into question" (1958: §133; original italics). This is mistaken if the aim is to stop us from asking honestly how things, broadly speaking, hang together. We ask because we want to know how we fit, broadly speaking, into the scheme of things. Whatever its mistakes and failures, the honest purpose of philosophy has always been to make this crisis of self-identity a little more explicit; but in education we face the same crisis, because it requires us to ask, in the same broad sense, what we should tell our children. It requires us to think for ourselves, standing at the altar of history, about the living wisdom of generations. The fundamental connection between education and philosophy is the crisis, deeply familiar and not at all, of coming to terms with reality.

Notes

1   This is notwithstanding the burgeoning literature in the field of philosophy of education. For more of the complaint I just made, cf. Bakhurst (2005: 261). The disciplinary issue is itself hardly new, at least in the Anglo-American philosophical tradition: Israel Scheffler, in his celebrated paper "Philosophy and the Curriculum," writes of "the old gulf between general philosophy and philosophy of education" (1970: 31).
2   Cf. Blake et al., who proceed to identify some of the new managerialism's familiar "watchwords," such as "skills, competences and techniques, flexibility, independence, targets and performance indicators, qualifications and credentials, learning outcomes" (2003: 8).
3   The most celebrated critique of the consignment of the educational endeavor to economic demands is J.-F. Lyotard's *The Postmodern Condition* (1984). For his analysis of the application of the "performativity principle" to education, cf. §12. It is jarring how correct his predictions have turned out to be. Paul Standish's *Beyond the Self* (1992) critically examines the surface language associated with the instrumental view in a classroom setting; cf. esp. Chapter 3.2, "Education and Myth"; and Appendix B, "The language of curriculum design." One example of the

new managerialism's effect on policy and language is the No Child Left Behind legislation of 2002 in the United States: "Although the ostensible purpose of the No Child Left Behind legislation was to close the achievement gap and provided equal learning opportunities for all students, the financial incentives and punishments associated with attaining Adequate Yearly Progress (AYP) goals have resulted in extreme pressure placed on teachers to ensure that their students succeed on their end-of-course tests. The outcome has been the encouragement of skill-based teaching strategies that are geared primarily toward success on these tests" (Milner et al. 2012: 5).

4   This is reminiscent of the comically, if depressingly, flat argument for the "universal application" or "transferability" of the "critical thinking skills" and "excellence in written and oral communication" supposedly gained through the study of the humanities in general and of philosophy in particular. That those who feel called to "the arts" can only defend their decisions by appeal either to an apparently global skillset or to what is "intrinsically," but elusively, valuable testifies to the extent to which the instrumental agenda pervades our thinking today. There is a bleaker social dimension, however: the student who graduates in the arts and humanities, and who cannot find an occupation that reflects her expertise, has in effect been pursuing her own selfish interests and in doing so has failed in her obligation to contribute to society at large. It is no wonder that the creative intellectual pursuits have been more or less absorbed into the sphere of commercial entertainment: the value of art and ideas is artificially generated through their production and consumption, but as such they are become instrumentally, not intrinsically, valuable.

5   "On behalf of the National Center for Education Statistics (NCES), I am pleased to present The Condition of Education 2020, an annual report mandated by the U.S. Congress that summarizes the latest data on education in the United States. This report uses data from across the center and from other sources and is designed to help policymakers and the public monitor educational progress. This year's report includes 47 indicators on topics ranging from prekindergarten through postsecondary education, as well as labor force outcomes and international comparisons" (Woodworth 2020: iii).

6   We might also add "pragmatist," since most or all forms of that view are explicitly anti-metaphysical; but I am sympathetic to the response, often deployed by Richard Rorty in defense of his American pragmatist approach, that nobody really believes relativism is true anyway, so lumping pragmatism and relativism together is misleading.

7   Blake et al. rightly perceive nihilistic attitudes in the new managerialism. Cf., e.g., xii: "Along with this reductionism comes a positive refusal to devote real thought to questions of the aims and purposes of education. It is striking that the official documents and reports of the last twenty or so years … declare that discussion of

ends and purposes is now redundant: a nostalgic practice which we have finally grown out of." I am not sure the authors acknowledge that there are forms of nihilism in the antifoundationalism I have outlined here. Although they begin by quoting Nietzsche's *The Will to Power*—"The highest values have devalued themselves"—they use this to draw attention to a "lack of commitment" in education in "much of the English-speaking world," where "[p]olitical programmes proceed under their own momentum" (2003: xi). They do, however, argue that there are "different guises nihilism can take" (57; cf. chapters 4–5).

8   "I never let my schooling get in the way of my education." This saying has been attributed, almost certainly falsely, to Mark Twain. More probably it derives from Grant Allen's *Post-Prandial Philosophy*: "What a misfortune it is that we should thus be compelled to let our boys' schooling interfere with their education!" (1894: 129)

9   What teachers need, perhaps, is time to ask openly about, and describe candidly, the very experience of teaching in a professional setting, and not only in the hallways during recess or at the pub on weekends. It is probably unsurprising that "professional development" days are commonly dreaded by teachers for being replete with make-work tasks and empty distractions cascading from the local school board administration—as though teachers cannot be trusted to be alone in their empty classrooms.

10 Cf., e.g., Hogan and Smith (2003). It is worth transcribing the following note from that paper: "Perhaps the example [i.e., of the resistance to theory in education] that best deserves to be remembered is a speech in 1991 by the then UK Secretary of State for Education, Kenneth Clarke: he described educational theory as 'barmy' and said teachers should ignore it" (180, n. 9).

11 I do not mean to downplay the problems posed by the new managerialism, or to imply that solutions to such problems are easy and neat. As I pointed out, both challenges to philosophy's significance to education are complementary with respect to their emphasis on practice; as such, they cannot ultimately be pulled apart and dealt with separately. I am, however, focusing here on the second, explicitly theoretical, attitude because it provokes worries that are closer to home for the philosophy of education.

12 This is not to say that no other animals exhibit patterns of behavior reminiscent both of education and language, but that education and language are characteristically human activities insofar as they occur on a scale undeniably more vast and complex than can be said for nonhumans, to the extent that humanity is itself defined by such activities. Whether this constitutes a metaphysical difference, for example, or how stark the difference may be, is a live issue to which I return in Chapter 2.

13 In the Preface he writes, "The whole sense of the book might be summed up in the following words: what can be said at all can be said clearly, and what we cannot talk about we must pass over in silence" (2007: 3).

14 As Hans-Georg Gadamer puts it, "In Wittgenstein, the problem of language is central from the very beginning, but even there it gains its full philosophical universality only as his thought matures" (1963: 173). For Gadamer, the mature Wittgenstein's really "decisive" idea is that "language is always right" (1962b: 126).

15 "Logic is not a body of doctrine, but a mirror-image of the world" (2007: §6.13).

16 In the *Tractatus*, Wittgenstein articulates this trinity by equating "the world" with "the totality of facts" (§1.1), "a fact" with a true "logical picture" of the world (§§2.19, 2.21), "a logical picture" with "a thought" (§3), and "a thought" with "a proposition with a sense" (§4), that is, a proposition that is "logically articulated" (§4.032).

17 "Propositions cannot represent logical form: it is mirrored in them. / What finds its reflection in language, language cannot represent. / What expresses itself in language, we cannot express by means of language. / Propositions show the logical form of reality. / They display it" (2007: §4.121).

18 "The propositions of logic demonstrate the logical properties of propositions by combining them so as to form propositions that say nothing" (2007: §6.121). "Contradiction, one might say, vanishes outside all propositions: tautology vanishes inside them. / Contradiction is the outer limit of propositions: tautology is the unsubstantial point at their center" (§5.143).

19 "There is no such thing as the subject that thinks or entertains ideas. ... The subject does not belong to the world: rather, it is a limit of the world. / Where *in* the world is a metaphysical subject to be found?" (§§5.631–5.633) Wittgenstein follows this up in §5.6331 with a diagram to remind us that, analogously, the eye itself does not appear in the visual field, but is one of its boundaries. He goes on, however, to suggest there is a "sense in which philosophy can talk about the self in a non-psychological way" (§5.641), as though he approves of such talk; but he does not, at least not strictly.

20 "Without philosophy thoughts are, as it were, cloudy and indistinct: its task is to make them clear and to give them sharp boundaries" (2007: §4.112). "The totality of propositions is language" (§4.001), and in inquiring after the truth about states of affairs, "Reality is compared with propositions" (§4.05). "The totality of true propositions," therefore, "is the whole of natural science (or the whole corpus of the natural sciences)" (§4.11).

21 Cora Diamond and James Conant (2004) advance a different reading of the *Tractatus*, called the Resolute Reading, and would take issue with this claim. For more of this discussion, cf. Kölbel and Weiss (2010).

22 Cf. Wittgenstein (2007: §6.211): "'What do we actually use this word or this proposition for?' repeatedly leads to valuable insights." Later, in the *Investigations*, he admonishes us to ask, "But how is this sentence applied—that is, in our everyday language? For I got it from there and nowhere else" (§134).

23 Cf. Wittgenstein (1958: §27): "'We name things and then we can talk about them: can refer to them in talk.'—As if what we did next were given with the mere act of naming. As if there were only one thing called 'talking about a thing'. Whereas in fact we do the most various things with our sentences. Think of exclamations alone, with their completely different functions. / Water! / Away! / Ow! / Help! / Fine! / No! / Are you inclined still to call these words 'names of objects'?" Cf. also this passage: "But how many kinds of sentence are there? Say assertion, question, and command?—There are *countless* kinds: countless different kinds of use of what we call 'symbols', 'words', 'sentences'. And this multiplicity is not something fixed, given once for all; but new types of language, new language-games, as we may say, come into existence, and others become obsolete and get forgotten. ... Review the multiplicity of language-games in the following examples, and in others: / Giving orders, and obeying them / Describing the appearance of an object, or giving its measurements / ... Play-acting / Singing catches / Guessing riddles / Making a joke; telling it / Solving a problem in practical arithmetic / Translating from one language into another / Asking, thanking, cursing, greeting, praying. / It is interesting to compare the multiplicity of the tools in language and of the ways they are used, the multiplicity of kinds of word and sentence, with what logicians have said about the structure of language. (Including the author of the *Tractatus Logico-Philosophicus*.)" (1958: §23)

24 That is, he gives up the belief that "sign and thing signified [must be] identical in respect of their total logical content" (1961: 4). True, "what we are aiming at is indeed *complete* clarity. But that simply means that the philosophical problems should *completely* disappear" (1958: §133). Cf. his comments, some of which are explicitly about the *Tractatus*, on "Elementary Propositions" in Appendix 4 of *Philosophical Grammar* (1974).

25 The example could be taken further: if the question remains what is meant by "brush," it might be thought necessary to cite, for example, the lengths of straw bound together with copper wire; but then "straw" and "copper wire" would also want analysis, so that a scientific examination of those materials would be in order, and so on down to the most primitive elements of physics; but then it would be absurd to suggest that what I mean when I say "My broom is in the corner" is actually "There is a conglomeration of such and such subatomic particles and quantum states arranged in such and such a way at such and such a location, belonging to me," according to the latest discoveries of physics; and anyway, relational terms like "bound," "together," "arranged," and "belonging" would also require analysis, and this could demand reference, sometimes negative, to other aspects of language, and they to yet others, so that my "meaning" just turns out to be an indefinite, perhaps infinite, array of propositions rather than simply "My broom is in the corner." This last point, as with the general direction

of Wittgenstein's example, illustrates something like the notion of "trace" as it appears in poststructuralist thought. An extended analysis like the above, however, still ignores the point of the original statement, that is, to answer to the question, "Where is your broom?"

26 Cf. Wittgenstein (1958: §18): "(And how many houses or streets does it take before a town begins to be a town?) Our language can be seen as an ancient city: a maze of little streets and squares, of old and new houses, and of houses with additions from various periods; and this surrounded by a multitude of new boroughs with straight regular streets and uniform houses."

27 The word "doxography" comes from the Greek *doxa* (belief, opinion) and *graphos* (writer), and describes the indirect way in which we understand the lives and ideas of historical figures whose works have not survived: that is, we only know of their ideas through the writings of others, just as our knowledge of Socrates derives mostly from Plato. Rorty's point is philosophers tend selectively to appropriate the ideas of others in order to fabricate grand philosophical narratives, perpetuating the notion that philosophical problems are real and universal.

28 I take the collective view of the editors to represent a generalized, but by no means all-encompassing, attitude. The philosophy of education literature is vast, and I am here only attempting to trace some of the main lines of thought with respect to the discipline's self-conception.

29 These are three of the most prominent philosophers in what has been referred to as the analytic philosophical movement in education; all three were affiliated with the Institute of Education in London, UK, a center of educational philosophical inquiry then and now. There were other major contributors, including Michael Oakeshott and Israel Scheffler, the latter of whom was at Harvard during the same period. Many of the relevant contributors to this movement can be found in the Routledge series International Library of the Philosophy of Education.

30 On the same page we find this: "It is abundantly clear nowadays that ultimately the crucially important questions of the curriculum are complex practical questions which no mere philosopher of education has a right to answer. ... On these technicalities, no mere philosopher is competent to pronounce" (1975: 1). Cf. also Peters (1975: vii–viii). There is, furthermore, Israel Scheffler's Introduction to his *Reason and Teaching*: "Educational practice, I am convinced, profits from the philosophical effort to crystallize and examine its basic concepts and guiding assumptions, while the scope of philosophical understanding is thereby enlarged. ... Nor is philosophy to be thought of as isolated from other studies bearing on educational practice. It is, to a large degree, in a 'second-order' position with respect to these other studies, concerned primarily, as it is, with their conceptual and methodological foundations. But its 'second-order' status implies neither superiority nor precedence; philosophy must respect the very studies that it aims to analyze, interpret, and criticize" (1973: 1–2).

31 Cf. Wittgenstein in the *Notebooks*: "I only want to justify the vagueness of ordinary sentences, for it *can* be justified" (1961: 70).

32 "The objectification of understanding is possible because commonly accepted criteria for using the terms [of public language] are recognized even if these are never explicitly expressed" (Hirst 1975: 39). This recalls Wittgenstein's early belief that "all the propositions of our everyday language, just as they stand, are in perfect logical order" (2007: §5.5563). I should note, however, that although the work of the London School was situated squarely in the analytic tradition, like much of that tradition it was not recklessly positivistic. Hirst, for example, recognizes in *Knowledge and the Curriculum* that "much of curriculum practice has simply 'grown' out of its social context" (1975: 10), even though he goes on to stress that "these factors in no way cast doubt on the logic of rational curriculum planning. Nor must the logic of the business be confused with an account of how, as a matter of fact, past and present curricula have come into being. … What we must do therefore is to make our curriculum planning progressively more rational by 'piecemeal engineering'" (11). Of course the last bit seems to, and in fact may, anticipate the eventual reorientation of Hirst's own thought. The lasting influence of Michael Oakeshott on Peters, Dearden, and Hirst also led to a significant amount of constructive work that went beyond the deadpan task of conceptual analysis, so that many new and valuable insights materialized. As Paul Standish put it to me once in conversation, the London School was perhaps more creative and insightful than it cared to admit.

33 I think it would be facile to try to categorize in any very strict way the "approaches" taken by particular philosophers of education, even when they themselves claim to favor a single procedure over every other. It is natural that many different approaches make an appearance in any given work, including prescription, proscription, therapy, conceptual clarification, deconstruction, speculation, logical deduction, metaphysical assertion, and so on. Moreover, the vast majority of educational philosophers cannot claim to have simply "done away with" the analytic approach: whether we like it or not, that approach continues to inform the literature in various ways, both helpful and unhelpful. My aim here is not to develop a neat taxonomy but to give a general indication of the form and aims of recent educational-philosophical discussion, so that I can identify the sense in which such discussion risks underestimating itself.

34 The difference is the totalizing clarity that has been analytic philosophy's trademark aim is absent. To think otherwise would be to imagine with the early Wittgenstein that although it is nonsense to try to articulate a metaphysical picture of language, it is still possible to make explicit all its grammatical rules and thereby bring to full transparency what can and cannot be said—to bring language to "a state of complete exactness" (1958: §91). It is worth acknowledging that the ordinary language philosophy of mid-twentieth-century Oxford, now seen as representing

the middle phase of analytic philosophy, could be called therapeutic, as could the corresponding work of the London School. Although Wittgenstein did influence the ordinary language tradition, however, the relationship was not straightforward: "So-called 'Ordinary Language Philosophy,' which flourished at Oxford mainly during the 1950s and which is chiefly associated with J. L. Austin, is sometimes thought to be a result of Wittgenstein's teachings, but in fact his influence was far less immediate than that; certainly Austin did not take himself to owe his ideas to Wittgenstein. ... Wittgenstein would have found aspects of 'Ordinary Language philosophy' uncongenial. None of the people who at that time were prominent in philosophy ... were Wittgensteinians; most of them were largely unaffected by Wittgenstein's later ideas, and some were actively hostile to them" (Grayling 1996: 128–9).

35 "Philosophy unravels the knots in our thinking; hence its result must be simple, but its activity as complicated as the knots it unravels" (Wittgenstein 2012: 1357). Note that the goal of therapy is not the aggressively skeptical one mentioned at the outset, of laying waste all ideals and ideologies governing educational practice. In fact such nihilistic "deconstructing without reconstructing" would run counter to the original idea of deconstruction as it appears in the works of, e.g., Jacques Derrida. I do not think anyone is seriously committed to that kind of project.

36 The Western philosophical tradition is, of course, replete with discussions about education: cf., e.g., Amélie O. Rorty (1998) and Steven Cahn (2009).

37 Cf., e.g., Conroy et al. (2008), R. A. Davis (2011), and Todd (2009).

38 For example, Andrew Davis need not claim that his critiques of assessment practices in England are always Wittgensteinian (cf., e.g., Davis 2013, 2014; but cf. Davis 2009), but in leveling those critiques he does, "broadly speaking," assume "the role of a conceptual therapist" (Davis 1998: 1). Harvey Siegel (e.g., 2008) and John White (e.g., 2007) might consider themselves largely opposed to either approach, while others like Paul Standish (1992, 1999; and cf. also Smeyers, Smith, and Standish 2007), David Bakhurst (2011), David Carr (1999), and the editors of the *Blackwell Guide* mentioned above (Blake et al. 2003) might promote both.

39 I leave this question open here, but return to it in Chapter 5.

40 Roughly the same thought finds expression in Donald Davidson's "On the Very Idea of a Conceptual Scheme," a conclusion of which is "that a form of activity that cannot be interpreted as language in our language is not speech behavior" (1974: 7).

41 Paul Fairfield discusses the idea of practice-immanent theorizing: "Theory can be conceived as arising from within practices themselves rather than descending on them from a transcendent location" (2011: 112). He continues on the next page: "In articulating criteria or principles already operative (prereflectively) in a practice, theory makes it possible to reorient, or even radically overhaul, the fashion in which it is conducted." The idea is that theory is supposed to belong to the practice

itself, arising from it and remaining true to it, whereas theorizing "from above" is liable to mislead: distortion "occurs, for example, when educators supplant aims that belong to the learning process with an agenda ... rather than cultivate the intellectual capacity of students" (113). Ruitenberg writes that the translational approach to the philosophy of education "transforms the relationship between theory and practice itself" (2010: 113). Compare Heidegger: "We measure deeds by the impressive and successful achievements of *praxis*. But the deed of thinking is neither theoretical nor practical, nor is it the conjunction of these two forms of behavior" (1947: 263).

42 "The appearance of the concept 'language' presupposes consciousness of language. But that is only the result of the reflective movement in which the one thinking has reflected out of the unconscious operation of speaking and stands at a distance from himself. The real enigma of language, however, is that we can never really do this completely. Rather, all thinking about language is already once again drawn back into language. We can only think in a language, and just this residing of our thinking in a language is the profound enigma that language presents to thought" (Gadamer 1966a: 62).

43 "Language is a labyrinth of paths. You approach from one side and know your way about; you approach the same place from another side and no longer know your way about" (Wittgenstein 1958: §203).

44 There are some exceptions. Cf., e.g., Naoko Saito's and Paul Standish's edited volume, *Stanley Cavell and the Education of Grownups*: "[It] is worth attending to Hilary Putnam's remark that Cavell is one of the few twentieth-century philosophers to explore the territory of 'philosophy as education'" (2012: 2). Cavell himself offers two contributions to that volume (2012a,b).

45 I owe this phrasing to my undergraduate professor, D. Anthony Larivière.

46 Israel Scheffler makes a similar point in his recent *Worlds of Truth*: "What is distinctive about philosophy is not its certainty but its comprehensive curiosity, not its infallibility but its interest in understanding every sphere of thought and life" (2009: 2). Cf. also this passage: "It seems to me that the proper scope of education is as large as civilization itself. The basic task of education, in my view, is to humanize and civilize, to introduce each generation afresh to all the great modes of human experience: to science and art, history and poetry, morality and religion, languages and philosophy. In this way, education serves to pass on the varied habits of mind that make up civilization and culture and, at the same time, to form the child into an autonomous participant in such culture" (60).

2

Education and Metaphysics: Being at Home in the World

The previous chapter was about philosophy's status with respect to education. Much of that discussion involved disciplinary matters. First, I tried to convey the predicament contemporary philosophers of education face if philosophy can no longer take itself to be marking out the foundations of discourse. I then outlined two broad approaches philosophers nevertheless see available—therapy and cultural politics. These, I claimed, are authentic insofar as they respect the ordinary integrity of education and welcome complexity, ambiguity, and a variety of perspectives in discourse, so that we can pretend to no final analysis or fixed theory of education.

At the end of the chapter, I attempted to recognize a yet deeper connection between education and philosophy, namely that the two are one in the unlimitedness of their interests and in their disregard for special territory. In other words, a significant part of their character involves the general crisis of self-identity, of coming to terms with reality. This will be a principal theme of the following chapters, and I expand on it here by exploring two related insights: that language is the medium of understanding; and that a distinguishing mark of humanity involves our understanding of ourselves as dwellers in a "world." These insights facilitate a general account—a philosophy—of education that would outline some of its fundamental achievements. In broad strokes the account is this. Over the course of her education, understood in the widest sense, a child learns language and so becomes minded: no longer just animal, she comes to be able to transcend her environment and exercise her powers of rationality by asking for and expressing reasons for thinking and doing; she comes to be able to think for herself and about herself in relation to the universe—able to philosophize, and to educate others in turn. Education thereby effects a transformation of monumental, indeed metaphysical, proportions.

Before developing these claims I address a concern, lingering from Chapter 1, about philosophy's ability to say anything fundamental about education.

Philosophy's Insights: Fundamental, Not Foundational

That education comprises the acquisition of mind through language is not only a metaphysical assertion: it is, I claim, an assertion about metaphysics, about its advent for the individual human being over the course of her education. Such talk naturally provokes apprehension. It can seem fraudulent to say that philosophy does not discover foundations, while maintaining that philosophy and education enjoy so fundamental a connection, which philosophy can illuminate by making metaphysical assertions. The concern is whether an idea can really be called "fundamental" yet not "foundational" in the traditional sense. This is a reasonable worry, one philosophers of education are likely to find substantial if they have embraced the "postmodern epistemology of discourse" outlined in Chapter 1; but I think reiterating another point made in that chapter can alleviate it.

There I concluded by arguing that philosophy stands on a different level of reflection than the other disciplines, because it is itself the "higher-level understanding" other disciplines partake of when they engage in self-reflection. I made the point by inverting the idea, attributable to Richard Rorty, that it would be possible to dissolve philosophy into the rest of academia, since philosophy claims no special territory. Instead, I suggested, this should help us see that philosophy arises everywhere as the general issue of self-understanding, of coming to terms with reality at large—something of equally deep significance for education. The idea of "levels of reflection" may mislead, however, insofar as it seems to encourage philosophy's continuing to pronounce on things from above or below. I am not advocating that; but at the same time, philosophical reflection is not just another theoretical perspective. We should rather understand philosophy as the exercise of self-understanding as such. This means treating it less strictly as a disciplinary approach and more as an explicitly self-conscious mode of thinking—and, in fact, of being.

Anticipating later chapters, let us modify the spatial metaphor. Recall Wilfrid Sellars's idea that philosophy asks about how things, broadly speaking, hang together (1963b: 1). Now we, those doing the asking, already find ourselves on the inside of what we are asking about; we think about things in general from the inside of things in general; and in doing so our view of things is liable to undergo transformation. Similarly, if the more fundamental discoveries of philosophy are called "foundational," it can only be in the sense of Wittgenstein's having discovered that the "foundation-walls are carried by the whole house" (1972: §248), or that the "river-bed of thoughts," which shapes the way we think, is itself shaped by the currents of thinking over time (1972: §§94–9). The practical changes brought about by such discoveries are not strategic recalculations based on new information, or groundbreaking methodologies founded on first principles. They are changes in attitude and in the character and lived quality of our activities—a reorientation to things in general.

If it is a mistake to characterize philosophy either as the ruler of discourse or as just another disciplinary approach among others, then it is doubly mistaken to do so regarding philosophy's relationship with education. Educators are called to say something about the world at large, to help children and pupils of all sorts to see how things generally fit together. Even if what they do is highly specific and seemingly indifferent to this general mission, the overall effect is to help bring the world into view for others. Educators do this from the inside of things, as particular beings in a particular historical context; and this adds profoundness to their everyday burden. The burden is profound not because educators have to try to transcend their human skin and talk about things from some divine perspective; what is profound is their undertaking to speak at all about the world, from inside their own skin, to and for others who live in skin too. In that sense, the task of education is fundamentally a philosophical one, and it would be worthwhile for educators to perceive this dimension in their workaday responsibilities. That does not mean all educators need formal training in philosophy, even though its study can prove life-changing. It is just to say that their understanding of, and reflecting upon, some of the deeper aspects of their own circumstances can profoundly impact their thinking and acting from day to day. The sort of educational philosophy I am recommending here—where education and philosophy belong fundamentally to one another, and where the basic aims and achievements of education are truly monumental—would aspire to the transformative self-understanding of educators in their humdrum daily activities. Philosophy sells itself short if it fails to recognize that it can still arrive at such insights—fundamental, though not foundational, to activities like education.

In Chapter 3, I look to etymology as a model for the kind of insight philosophy can yield, and to help improve our understanding of education's achievements. That argument, however, turns on a view of the relationship between mind and language, which I am about to present here. In the coming sections, I suggest that our partaking of the understanding that language affords distinguishes us humans from other sorts of beings, and that the broad aim of education is therefore the formation of reason through language. Later I will argue that education effects the advent of metaphysics for the individual by cultivating her ability to think about reality in general; and this will lead back to my earlier claim that education and philosophy belong to one another in a fundamental way.

Human and NonHuman Animals and the Language of Rationality

What do we mean when we talk about mindedness as distinctively human? That our ability to think differentiates us from other animals has long been accepted without much controversy.[1] Aristotle points to the rational principle, to "the power of thinking, i.e. mind," in arguing that humans belong to a different class of animals, which in turn belong to a special order of living things: humans stand at the end of a tripartite grouping of "powers" of increasing complexity, beginning with the purely nutritive, as with a plant; extending through the appetitive, sensory, and locomotive in addition to the nutritive, as with a lion; and on to the rational in addition to those other powers, all of which together only humans possess (*De Anima* II.3; 415a7–10).[2] As Sebastian Rödl puts it, "To be, for a living being, is to live; to live, for a human being, is to think" (2020: 290). In light of empirical studies in animal psychology, however, there has lately been more resistance to the idea that human beings alone exhibit rationality.[3] It can thus appear that yet another tired philosophical theory has been overturned by natural science; but that is mistaken, and it will be helpful to understand why.

The more we insist on a rigid conceptual distinction between humans and their activities and nonhuman animals and their activities, the more difficult it will be to retain its salience in questionable circumstances of the kind empirical studies routinely uncover. Examples have arisen and in some cases abound, in the animal kingdom, of complex social interaction, emotional states, rule breaking, problem solving, tool use, gesturing, dialect, and visual self-recognition; more domestically, it is difficult not to describe a pet as having a certain kind of personality. That it makes sense to talk like this, however, is already in harmony with the later Wittgenstein's insight about language: only family resemblance, not a special set of criteria, moderates the appropriate application of concepts; language takes care of itself and resists being fixed by analysis. This in turn can seem at odds with the presumed goals of natural science, including a complete taxonomy of the physical universe. To say that language takes care of itself, however, is not to suggest we stop investigating the similarities and differences between humans and other animals. It is to insist that our understanding the distinction does not require us to ascribe every living being, habit of activity, fragment of behavior, brain region, and neural signal from any time and place into one or another category—rational or nonrational—as though if "rationality" cannot tolerate binary application, so much the worse for that concept.

The problem with a rigid conceptual distinction between humans and nonhumans that is based on the rational principle does not lie in the distinction itself, but in its rigidity. It is a mistake to think concepts like rationality are worthless, or that their value is in deferral, until scientifically defined. If we believe Wittgenstein, we can say such concepts are important because, as part of the riverbed of our thoughts, they constitute the generally stable background against which our thinking and investigating have any meaning at all: yet they also exhibit a kind of versatility, allowing their meaning and application to shift over time.

We can therefore ask whether studies in animal cognition are in the business of disproving the quasi-scientific theories of old, or whether they simply revalue original philosophical insights in new and exciting ways. We can wonder whether the question about animal cognition could have arisen if a notion like rationality were not appropriately versatile. Wittgenstein learned that clarity is not a necessary result of restricted language. We learn too by exploring old ideas in new ways. Language is resilient, fundamentally open to the new. It allows us to transform our understanding by relating the unfamiliar to the familiar, even if vastly removed from us personally, psychologically, culturally, biologically, geographically, historically, or in some other way. Likewise it is possible to imagine that animals exhibit certain forms of rational behavior without having to imagine that they are in full possession of the rational principle, as humans are, or that the idea of rationality as a distinctively human power becomes less salient when understood in terms of its versatility.

Language as the Medium of Understanding

If these reflections about the language of animal psychology sound plausible, it should lend credence to the idea that language and thought are inextricably related—or as Hans-Georg Gadamer puts it, "that understanding is inseparable from language and that language is related to reason of every kind" (2004b: 469). No doubt language is a going concern in our everyday activities, and no doubt our understanding is affected by the words and concepts we see available in a situation; but more than that, language is the threshing floor of thinking, the natural medium of our understanding. This is a comparatively recent insight that can appear both obvious and profound, and it has lived up to itself in transforming the original notion of rationality as a distinctively human power.

Empirically speaking, the power of language seems about equally distinctive of humans as the power of rationality, and this is no accident. The presence and character of linguistic behavior dominate our judging the reasonableness of conduct, and we articulate those judgments in language.[4] After returning from a morning of fishing, we might wonder aloud why the fishing lodge's legendary owner, Vic Beckel, suddenly exclaims and sprints to the boat slips—irregular behavior for someone normally so composed.

> "He forgot to replace the drain plug," someone answers.
> "How do you know?"
> "It was buried somewhere beneath all those expletives you heard."

We can recognize Vic's odd behavior as rational by piecing together his abbreviated explanation with his actions. Even if Vic had said nothing, his explanation upon returning would set us at ease.

This may seem to ignore the possibility that language is just a chance mechanism allowing already rational animals to communicate the cleverness of their behavior, but language is profoundly constitutive of that cleverness and that rationality, and shapes it constantly. Suppose Vic cannot find his drain plug, and his boat is actually sinking at the dock.

> Someone hollers, "There's an extra plug in the Gun Motor Room, by the marine batteries!"
> "Check my radio box," offers another.
> Vic replies, "Get one—I'm going to take the boat out and drain it. I'll meet you at the main dock in a few minutes."
> "What if you can't get up on step?"
> "I didn't eat breakfast."
> "What?"
> "Nothing, never mind."

Here is language at work, rationally affecting behavior; but it too is behavior that is rational, affected in turn by the behavior of others. Through verbal communication we think out loud with one another about states of affairs, and the states of affairs themselves draw out our responses to them, inviting our rational participation. Language is the direct way in which we can ask about and recommend ways of thinking, speaking, and acting. "Reaching an understanding in language places a subject matter before those communicating like a disputed object set between them" (Gadamer 2004b: 443). Our mutual interest is how best to understand and cope with our situation.

The ubiquity and importance of language in our lives only seems astonishing if we fail to recognize language and reason as conceptually conjoined. If we understand rational behavior from the outset as oriented by meanings explainable in language—so that the perpetrator can in principle recognize, explain, and debate the meaning of what he thinks, says, and does—then of course language belongs together with the rational principle. Humans represent themselves as acting rationally all the time, and they do that rationally too—in language. That is part of our form of life, and it permeates how we live in a way that sets us apart from other animals.

To present language as the medium of understanding is not, however, to put it at the top of some hierarchy of meaningfulness, so that only the written symbol or the spoken word is truly meaningful in a way that a broken hand, sex, or a bone striking a bodhrán are not.[5] It is just that questions about the meaningfulness of things arise in language and get pursued in it, by beings for whom language is a central life activity. The entirety of our existence is available to language, promising what Gadamer calls "an ever-possible verbalization" (2004a: 551). Language is the medium of thought in that it carries us through in all stages of understanding and misunderstanding, for any subject matter: a saying, some written text or mathematical equation, a piece of art, or some other artifact like a tool or technique; or something from our natural environment, like the brightness of the stars or the effect of a hard northwest wind on the fishing; anything in the world. Language is the space where understanding becomes a live issue: it is the threshing floor, not the terminus, of meaning, and we all share in the work of winnowing possibilities and harvesting truth. "[L]anguage has its true being only in dialogue, in *coming to an understanding*. Coming to an understanding ... is a life process in which a community of life is lived out ... [and] 'world' is disclosed" (Gadamer 2004b: 443; original italics).

Thus "the speculative structure of language emerge[s], not as the reflection of something given but as the coming into language of a totality of meaning" (Gadamer 2004b: 469). In language our situation comes into view not prearranged, but as something to be explored. This inception of possibility is due to language's "free universality," its versatility in judging one thing on the basis of another, as Gadamer points out happens in analogy:

> [In analogy] the dialectical capacity of discovering similarities and seeing one quality common to many things is still very close to the free universality of language and its principles of word formation. ... Transference from one sphere to another not only has a logical function; it corresponds to the fundamental metaphoricity of language.
>
> (429)

That last phrase contrasts deeply with the science-oriented, positivist picture of language Wittgenstein presented in his early thinking and which he later deconstructs. On that picture, the purpose of language is to communicate readymade thoughts and facts as clearly as possible. Gadamer's insight here is comparable to the views of the later Wittgenstein. It is that the "living metaphoricity of language" (431)—its "essential inexactness" and "variability" (435), its constant analogizing—already stands behind the very idea of distinguishing by logical analysis between the "*proper* and the *metaphorical* meaning of a word. What originally constituted the basis of the life of language and its logical productivity, the spontaneous and inventive seeking out of similarities "by means of which it is possible to order things," is now marginalized and instrumentalized into a rhetorical figure called metaphor" (431; original italics). Language is no mere means of communication. Rather "the advance work of language" (429), which is fundamentally versatile and part of the ongoing life activity of its speakers, is logically prior to anything like formal logic and "the scientific ideal of unambiguous designation," alongside which "the life of language itself continues unchanged" (432).

Gadamer's legacy is based on his "revival of the expression *hermeneutics*"— the art and theory of understanding—and on his giving it "philosophic" significance by asking after "all human experience of the world and human living" (2004b: xxv–xxvii; original italics). He understands language as a constant play of meanings, circling hermeneutically from one thing to another and from general to particular and back again, always involving an interpreter in the act of interpretation. It is well known that the word "metaphor" is itself a metaphor, from the Greek meaning "to carry over." Language's "fundamental metaphorical nature" (428) plays out constantly by "carrying over" meaning from here to there and there to here. The result is this "widening experience" (428) of the understanding—the outward-spiraling enrichment of our encounter with the world, with which we are all familiar and for which the "intimate unity of speech and thought" (431) is essential.

Language as the Repository of Historical Mind

To illustrate the intimate relation of language and thought I have emphasized language's versatility and its power to facilitate creative change in what we think, say, and do; but the "advance work" of language also bears directly on the origins of rationality in the individual, hence on the very idea of education. Language facilitates new understanding for grownup thinkers, but it also stands ready to enable a child's understanding *per se* as the living embodiment of the thinking of her elders and ancestors. To that extent we can call language the repository of historical mind.

A recent proponent of the view that language is distinctive of the human power of rationality, and permeates our mode of living, is John McDowell. At the end of *Mind and World* he offers a very general account of education, in the broadest sense, centering on language. Throughout his book he borrows the term "space of reasons" from Wilfrid Sellars to describe the rational dimension of human living; he also uses the term *Bildung*[6]—borrowed from Gadamer and the German philosophical tradition—to refer to the maturation of humans into and through this dimension:

> Now it is not even clearly intelligible to suppose a creature might be born at home in the space of reasons. Human beings are not: they are born mere animals, and they are transformed into thinkers and intentional agents in the course of coming to maturity. This transformation risks looking mysterious. But we can take it in our stride if, in our conception of the *Bildung* that is a central element in the normal maturation of human beings, we give pride of place to the learning of language. In being initiated into a language, a human being is introduced into something that already embodies putatively rational linkages between concepts, putatively constitutive of the layout of the space of reasons, before she comes on the scene. ... Human beings mature into being at home in the space of reasons or, what comes to the same thing, living their lives in the world; we can make sense of that by noting that the language into which a human being is first initiated stands over against her as a prior embodiment of mindedness, of the possibility of an orientation to the world.
>
> (1994: 125)

Cultivating a home in the space of reasons is the same as developing the power of rationality, the freedom of thought and action invoked by Aristotle's rational principle; but McDowell rightly associates this development with learning a language—not any one in particular, but some language or other. Here a child is introduced first of all to "a repository of tradition, a store of historically accumulated wisdom about what is a reason for what" (126), and is thereby transformed into a thinker. Another word for this process is "education."[7]

It is important that McDowell invokes the notion of a repository—a place of resource. It recalls Wittgenstein's description of language as the riverbed of our thoughts, a sort of gradual sedimentation of the currents of thinking which shapes thinking in turn. Here is that passage from *On Certainty*:

> I did not get my picture of the world by satisfying myself of its correctness ...
> No: it is the inherited background against which I distinguish between true and false.
> The propositions describing this world-picture might be part of a kind of mythology. ...

> It might be imagined that some propositions ... were hardened and functioned as channels for such ... propositions as were not hardened but fluid; and that this relation altered with time, in that fluid propositions hardened and hard ones became fluid.
> The mythology may change back into a state of flux, the river-bed of thoughts may shift. But I distinguish between the movement of the waters on the river-bed and the shift of the bed itself; though there is not a sharp division of the one from the other. ...
> And the bank of that river consists partly of hard rock, subject to no alteration or only to an imperceptible one, partly of sand, which now in one place now in another gets washed away, or deposited.
>
> (1972: §§94–7, 99)

Wittgenstein describes the view of the world that language affords as the "inherited background" giving sense to a person's thought. As a tradition of thought it stands in advance of the individual, but is itself susceptible to change—a riverbed whose waters alter its shape. While McDowell supplements "repository" with "store" in his illustration of the same phenomenon, we can maintain Wittgenstein's aquatic metaphor and shift its emphasis by saying language is the "source" or "fountain" of understanding—its "origin"—as well as the site of its accretion. In any case, language takes on a dual character. It does not only represent the gradual formation of thinking, as "a life process in which a community of life is lived out." It is the wellspring of conceptual resources for rational behavior, available to individuals just waking to the world through education.

Here education reveals itself as fundamentally an event of language. First, through initiation into language an individual becomes a thinking being, at all: language is the historical embodiment of mind; so in learning her first language a person comes to partake of the thinking that the language embodies, learning to think for herself in the manner of its speakers. Second, the idea of introduction or initiation suggests the learning this involves is not so much didactic, in the sense of acquiring belief in a sequence of true propositions, as holistic: Wittgenstein writes, "When we first *believe* anything, what we believe is not a single proposition, it is a whole system of propositions. (Light dawns gradually over the whole)" (1972: §141).[8] Third, the historical tradition that language embodies is a putatively rational inheritance, so it is subject to criticism and change over time. Finally, the notion of language as a repository of culture and history implies that learning to think is a sociohistorical process requiring the setting of culture and the active involvement of its members—elders, caregivers, educators, peers.

Education as Transformation

Missing from this is a clear vision of how a child's learning language constitutes a transformation of metaphysical proportions. In *The Formation of Reason*, David Bakhurst takes up McDowell's general picture, developing an account of education as the formation of mind through initiation into the space of reasons, where the child comes to be at home as a rationally free, self-conscious individual. Bakhurst calls this the "transformational view" in deference to McDowell's remark, quoted above, that "[h]uman beings ... are born mere animals, and they are transformed into thinkers and intentional agents in the course of coming to maturity" (1994: 125; cf. Bakhurst 2014).

Bakhurst's task is explicitly philosophical, and positively so. It is "not just to observe the importance" of the transformative character of education in anticipation of "a genuine theoretical account," but "to elucidate the concepts that will enable us to *think* its importance"—concepts like "person, rationality, the space of reasons, mindedness, thought, meaning, normativity, agency, second nature, and so on" (2011: 10; original italics). In the spirit of McDowell and ultimately of Wittgenstein, this often involves disarming traditional philosophical worries about such concepts. The attempt, however, is not just to calm anxieties therapeutically, or to engage in cultural politics about education from a philosophical perspective; nor is it to delineate the foundations of a grand philosophy of education. The intent is to say something conceptually fundamental about education, but only by "drawing attention to facts of human development that are in plain view," in a way that is alive to the varieties and complexities of that development in a sociohistorical context (10).[9]

The idea of a transformation of a "mere animal" into a "thinker" depends on a conceptual distinction between the two. Bakhurst, following McDowell, articulates this transformation as the emergence of a "second nature," where an individual comes to be at home in the space of reasons—able to recognize the meaningfulness and reasonableness of all sorts of things and to partake of that meaningfulness in language: in short, to behave in a meaning-oriented way. Such a transformation is only available to human beings because of our comparatively expansive developmental capacities and our sociohistorical form of life, in and through which language has emerged over time as their vital embodiment. Second nature is to be distinguished from first nature, the purely animal character of our biological being. The transformation, then, is of an individual possessing a first, animal nature who acquires a second, rational nature through initiation by others into that prior embodiment of mind called language. Through the linguistic happening that is education a "mere animal" transforms into a rationally free being by acquiring a second nature.[10]

The rigidity of the distinction between "mere animals" and "rational animals" is particularly sensitive for the transformational view. Depending on one's attitude about the distinction, the transformational view can seem incoherent from contrary directions. Addressing these two objections will allow for a fuller account of the transformational view to emerge.

Objection 1: "Transformation" Is Mysterious

The first concern is that the position is unduly anthropocentric and exceptionalist, according the human species an unfounded, and excessively intellectualized, pride of place over other animals. In *Mind and World*, for example, McDowell writes, "Dumb animals are natural beings and no more. Their being is entirely contained within nature" (1994: 70). This can sound plainly wrong. McDowell uses the word "dumb" literally, but describing the human power of rationality in contrast to an entirely natural mode of being can make it seem that rationality transcends nature in some occult way, as a soul might be thought to transcend a body. It also appears blind to the good sense of applying certain descriptions to animal behavior that are reminiscent of the emotional, social, and intellectual complexities of human behavior. Finally, the suggestion of two realms separated by a conceptual chasm seems to disrespect the obviously gradual transition to rational maturity in normal human development; and a mature human would have to span the chasm in an ultimately mysterious way. The worry is therefore that any substantial distinction between the animal and the rational, between our first and second natures, is going to preclude a transformation from one to the other.

In response, Bakhurst reminds us how we recognize a child's gradually emerging mindedness in the first place:

> The infant's elders must see in her the potential for reason. Where are they to find it except in the form taken by the child's animal being? What they must find meaning in is precisely her physical engagement with her surroundings. Reflection on the interaction of infant and parent, in search of a meeting of minds, makes evident how artificial it is to separate the child's emerging mindedness from the specific character of her bodily presence in the world. This enables us to see personhood as a fundamental modification of the mode of life activity of an animal, a human being.
>
> (2011: 62)

The plain reality of a child's development solves the mystery. What is in plain view here is the fact of a child, a particular physical being, who from birth immediately begins to interact with her physical surroundings. She is animate—alive, breathing, alert. Gradually her elders and caregivers recognize and encourage, in the way she behaves, her emerging mental capacities. She is naturally responsive to this encouragement. She begins to develop fluency interacting with those in her vicinity, building with them intersubjectivity, and eventually developing language, which enables her to think and speak. She learns to think and speak by learning to think and speak like her elders. Having responded, as it were, to the call of mind, eventually she herself becomes a full-fledged member of her community, someone who can play the role of elder and caregiver in turn, who can represent the community and speak on its behalf, and even criticize its practices.

Nothing about this normal development is occult or supernatural. The child's emerging rationality manifests in her animal presence and activity in relation to her sociohistorical surroundings: it is "present in action, rather than simply standing behind bodily movement" (Bakhurst 2011: 64). It becomes second nature for the child to recognize and respond to the meaningfulness of things, to be "moved by meanings" (17–18).[11] Her behavior takes on a rational character, reflective of a certain kind of animal—a human one, because that is what she is.[12]

Rising to "World"

It is important to reflect on what is meant by "merely animal" behavior. If the rational behavior of a person is supposed to be a manifestation of her animality, what is the animal without the rational? What is the child prior to her education—what is it for her to be born an animal, possessing only a first, biological nature, before she acquires a second, rational one? McDowell recalls (1994: 115–19), and Bakhurst affirms (2011: 158–62), a way of describing the merely animal presented by Gadamer in *Truth and Method*. In short, animals live in an environment, whereas humans inhabit a world:

> In mere animals, sentience is in the service of a mode of life that is structured exclusively by immediate biological imperatives. ... [W]e can recognize that a merely animal life is shaped by goals whose control of the animal's behavior at a given moment is an immediate outcome of biological forces. A mere animal does not weigh reasons and decide what to do. Now Gadamer's thesis is this: a life that is structured only in that way is led not in the world, but only in an environment. For a creature whose life has only that sort of shape, the milieu

it lives in can be no more than a succession of problems and opportunities, constituted as such by those biological imperatives.

(McDowell 1994: 115)

The lives of animals are "entirely contained within nature" insofar as the impact of their environment on their behavior is relatively immediate and inflexible. That is not to say a lion cannot choose how best to attack the gazelle it senses downrange, or exhibit veteran patience and ingenuity in doing so; but its motivations with respect to the gazelle, and the motivations of both of them in relation to each other and their environment, are not possible objects of reflection for either animal. Such reflection would imply degrees of freedom and intellectual distance from the situation that are simply unavailable. "Animals can leave their environment and move over the whole earth without severing their environmental dependence" (Gadamer 2004b: 442).

By contrast, humans experience *"rising to 'world'* itself, to true environment," adopting "another posture toward it" through the development of language (Gadamer 2004b: 442; original italics). McDowell glosses Gadamer's thought:

> To acquire the spontaneity of the understanding [i.e., "deciding what to think and do"] is to become able, as Gadamer puts it, to "rise above the pressure of what impinges on us from the world"—that succession of problems and opportunities constituted as such by biological imperatives—into a "free, distanced orientation." And the fact that the orientation is free, that it is above the pressure of biological need, characterizes it as an orientation to the world. For a perceiver with capacities of spontaneity, the environment is more than a succession of problems and opportunities; it is the bit of objective reality that is within her perceptual and practical reach. It is that for her because she can conceive it in ways that display it as that.
>
> (1994: 116, citing Gadamer 2004b: 441–2)

McDowell admits in a footnote that "Gadamer's topic ... is the role of language in disclosing the world to us; it is language ... that makes the 'free distanced orientation' possible. ... [M]eanwhile I adapt Gadamer's remarks to my purposes" (1994: 116, n. 6). McDowell's omission may be excusable, but ours would not.[13] Humans are distinct, Gadamer argues, in that we partake of Aristotle's principle of rationality, the intellectual freedom to transcend various demands placed on us by our surroundings; but this "free, distanced orientation ... is always realized in language" (2004b: 442). Gadamer's main influence here is his teacher, Martin Heidegger, who had already connected freedom explicitly to language: "Because plants and animals are lodged in their respective environments but are never placed freely in the clearing of Being which alone is 'world,' they lack language" (Heidegger 1947: 230).[14]

Language's "free universality" is what affords us the freedom to transcend our environment and rise to "world." Even the communication of animals remains severely confined, whereas the versatility of language reveals the world as such and frees us toward it.

> Indeed, human language takes place in signs that are not rigid, as animals' expressive signs are, but remain variable, not only in the sense that there are different languages, but also in the sense that within the same language the same expression can designate different things and different expressions the same thing.
> (Gadamer 1966a: 60)

> Animals ... make themselves understood, but not about matters of fact, the epitome of which is the world. ... Whereas the call of animals induces particular behavior in the members of the species, men's coming to a linguistic understanding with one another through the logos reveals the existent itself.
> (Gadamer 2004b: 442)

Of course in coming to a linguistic understanding of the world we do so in a way that does not delete or forsake our animal being or our environment, "as if being human exempted one from having to be somewhere in particular" (McDowell 1994: 118). As Bakhurst points out, the rational freedom exhibited in human behavior cannot be understood apart from that being and that environment. In fact, according to Gadamer, "environment" originally described "the purely human world"—"the 'milieu' in which man lives, and [whose] importance consists in its influence on his character and way of life. ... In a broad sense, however, this concept can be used to comprehend all conditions on which a living creature depends" (2004b: 441). What becomes clear from this is that there is indeed something special about the way we live. We, "unlike all other living creatures, [have] a 'world', for other creatures do not in the same sense have a relationship to the world, but are, as it were, embedded in their environment" (441). Language provides the intellectual distance from our environment needed for so many varieties of possible action and ways of thinking to come up in reflection.[15] In language we live in the world and are oriented toward it as such, as a space of meanings and possibilities profoundly influenced by the environment we inhabit.

The behavior of nonhuman animals, possessing powers of self-movement, sentience, and so on, cannot be understood as other than that of a physical life form. Despite those powers, they do not have the freedom to transcend the biological demands placed on them in the way that we can. This is not, however, "to imply that features of the environment are nothing to a perceiving animal.

… Exactly not: we need to appeal to an animal's sensitivity to features of its environment if we are to understand its alert and self-moving life, the precise way in which it copes competently with its environment" (McDowell 1994: 117). We understand the lives of nonhuman animals precisely by appeal to those modes of being we share with them. Animal powers of coping can be considered a kind of proto-subjectivity: language allows for such talk because it is versatile, but most such descriptions will be in "proto" form. Clearly there is a family resemblance between the activities and behaviors of nonhuman animals and those of rational animals; but in applying distinctively human concepts to such phenomena we should still appreciate the real differences between the rational and the nonrational.

To describe animals as living in an environment, and humans as coming to inhabit a world by learning language, is a way of maintaining sight of those differences: "The world as world exists for man as for no other creature that is in the world" (Gadamer 2004b: 440). To be at home in the space of reasons is to be at home in the world as such, to be minded, and that happens through education in the broadest sense.

Objection 2: "Transformation" Disrespects the Metaphysical Distinction

There is an opposing worry about the transformational view, which brings into focus the idea of education as effecting a metaphysical change. The contention, put forward by Sebastian Rödl in a paper entitled "Education and Autonomy," is that the conceptual distinction between animal and human must remain rigid, but at the expense of a metaphysical transformation from one to the other: "A human being is said to have a first nature and a second nature, being an animal in virtue of the first, a person in virtue of the second. He has no nature that embraces his first and his second nature, making them one nature" (2016: 87). This, Rödl thinks, "disrespects the depth to which reason defines the human being" (87) in its "metaphysical" form, a form that awakens only in the sociohistorical setting (87–8; see also 95–6).

Rödl thinks the idea of a child who is born a mere animal, and who changes into a person, is incoherent. He tries to show this by considering a fictional but analogous transformation just one level down on Aristotle's tripartite distinction of living beings (2016: 87–8). Rödl imagines a being called a "mion," an animal very much like a lion but born without the ability to exercise any of its animal capacities whatsoever, not even sense perception. Through weeks of being constantly licked by its parents, the mion gradually awakens to its powers of sentience, locomotion, and so on. If the mion's parents fail to lick the youngster adequately, it perishes. For Rödl, it is absurd to say the mion is born a plant and transforms into an animal: no, it is born an animal and comes to exercise the powers natural to its species, thereby living up to its form as an animal of a certain kind, a mion. Analogously, a human is not born a mere animal, becoming human through education: she is a person already in possession of the powers available to her as a member of the human species, who through education learns from others the habit of exercising those powers. This satisfies the idea that education is nothing more or less than "the child's growth into itself" (87).

In a way, of course, Rödl is perfectly right. Even the infant must be apprehended in her metaphysical form, and that form is defined in terms of Aristotle's rational principle. "[E]ducation's role … is the formation of something always-already there, not its creation" (Bakhurst 2014: 318).[16] Rödl's example also reinforces the idea that a child is born into a sociohistorical setting as "an already going concern," to use McDowell's phrase. A child's identity and potential for rational behavior are fundamentally related to this.

On the other hand, Rödl's analogy is incomplete. To be fully analogous to the human situation, we would have to say that a mion whose parents failed to awaken its animal powers in the right way need not perish, but could continue to exist in a vegetative state, subsisting in a way reminiscent of a plant. That sounds coherent, or at least as coherent as saying that a feral child brought up completely without human contact, say by a pack of wolves, need not perish but could survive as an animal—one which, unfortunately, remains unable to exercise those powers of rational freedom once available to her in her developmental phase.[17] As Kant puts it, "Man can only become man by education. He is merely what education makes of him" (1960: 6). Without education, a person cannot be alive to the meaningfulness of things as they find expression in the language of a human culture; but that is just because she lives entirely without that culture; but she is not therefore dead. To reinterpret McDowell, then, a child without education remains a mere animal by remaining alive, breathing, alert—but unable to exercise her full and natural, human powers of rationality. Education in the broadest sense transforms a child's life by orienting her toward meaning. It opens her up to the world as such, not just to the challenges and opportunities of her immediate environment.

This is to take a view of the transformation effected by education as one that is indeed metaphysical, but not in the sense Rödl understands it to be, namely, from one species to another; but nor is it anything occult. McDowell writes,

> We should not be frightened away from holding that initiation into the right sort of communal practice makes a *metaphysical* difference ... Responsiveness to reasons ... marks out a fully-fledged human individual as no longer a merely biological particular, but a being of a metaphysically new kind.
>
> (2009b: 172; original italics)

The metaphysical difference that education effects is the formation of reason. A child comes to be at home in the world and in the space of reasons, so that her animal being takes on a self-conscious, rational orientation. Her new orientation comes with her recognizing the meaningfulness of the language behavior of her peers, elders, and ancestors—and of the world in which they live and about which they speak.

Education as Effecting the Advent of Metaphysics in the Individual

I have been exploring the idea that education effects the gradual transformation of a human being from a mere animal into one that is able to recognize, express, and respond to meanings and reasons in language. In this broad sense the result of education is distinctively human mindedness. The notion of a transformation depends on a conceptual distinction between a merely animal mode of being and a human mode of being; but neither the distinction nor the transformation from one to the other should be seen as occult or supernatural. Through language a child realizes her powers of thought and thereby acquires a sense of herself as living in the world. Language, in turn, is versatile: its "free universality" allows us to partake of the "ever-widening experience" of understanding. It allows us to talk about what the educative transformation is like, in a way that respects the real similarities and real differences that can be found among human and nonhuman animals.

I conclude by exploring further the metaphysical significance of this transformation. I have argued that what is metaphysical about it is not that it is a change from one kind of creature to another: it is a change from one mode of being to another, from living in an environment to living in the world as such. This is a profound, but not occult, way of describing the normal development of humans: over the course of her maturation, a vulnerable infant grows into a fully fledged thinking being. She comes to terms with reality "literally" just as well as "metaphorically": for her, the world comes to presence as such through language.

A thinking being is a metaphysical being in that she can think about reality at large, about the arrangement and even the meaning of things in general. She can think about the world and articulate it as that, transcending her environment in a way other animals do not. She is at home in the world, even if she is also not at home insofar as she senses the uncanniness of being at all. The capacity for thinking gives rise to a crisis of self-identity, that profound anxiety about what or who one is, or what it means to be anything—or why there is anything in the first place, rather than nothing. That sort of anxiety, a kind of indeterminate anxiety with respect to reality at large, is what Martin Heidegger in his famous lecture entitled "What is Metaphysics?" calls "being held out into the nothing" (1929: 103). He takes this to be an experience original to humans: the possibility of anxiety about things in general defines human subjectivity, what he calls "Dasein," or "being-in-the-world." "Holding itself out into the nothing, Dasein is in each case already beyond beings as a whole. This being beyond beings we call 'transcendence'" (103).

To experience the anxiety of "being held out into the nothing" or "being beyond beings" is to recognize a crisis. It is to experience a kind of profound anguish, dread, or strangeness in response to the very idea of being a thinking being who thinks about the generality of things. It is not a merely pathological response, however. Such anxiety is a kind of "attunement" (1929: 100) to the world and to "beings as a whole," an orientation to reality at large. An analogous experience is the profound one of loving and being loved by someone, of loving and being loved by another "being beyond beings." Like existential dread, love is not just a feeling: it reveals the world as a whole to us in our basic orientation to it. The pure and simple joy of love—of being attuned to one another as one, the world be what it may—is something that locates us together in the world profoundly. "Such being attuned, in which we 'are' one way or another and which determines us through and through, lets us find ourselves among beings as a whole" (100). In love we find something like absolute safety, and perhaps that is after all the proper answer to the anxious and solitary questioning of "being held out into the nothing"; but in either case one is attuned to the world in general, is oriented toward it.[18]

Already a profound influence on Gadamer, Heidegger's thinking about "being in the world" as "being held out into the nothing" directly informs this chapter's discussion. Insofar as education develops our capacity to transcend our environment in a way that gives us an orientation to the world, we can recognize ourselves as rising "beyond beings as a whole." We rise to "world" as such, and that means to the rational freedom that is involved in self-consciousness; but that in turn is for us to recognize ourselves as metaphysical beings.

> If in the ground of its essence Dasein were not transcending, which now means, if it were not in advance holding itself out into the nothing, then it could never be related to beings or even to itself.
> Without the original revelation of the nothing, no selfhood and no freedom.
> (1929: 103)

Our inquiry concerning the nothing is to bring us face to face with metaphysics itself. The name "metaphysics" derives from the Greek *meta ta physika*. This peculiar title was later interpreted as characterizing the inquiry, the *meta* or *trans* extending out "over" beings as such.

> Metaphysics is inquiry beyond or over beings, which aims to recover them as such and as a whole for our grasp.
> (106)

Going beyond beings occurs in the essence of Dasein. But this going beyond is metaphysics itself. ... Metaphysics is the basic occurrence of Dasein. It is Dasein itself.

(109)

If we can acquiesce in a conception of metaphysics as "being in the world" by "going beyond beings," then to say that education effects a metaphysical transformation is just to say that a physical being becomes a metaphysical being precisely in the sense of recognizing herself as a being in the world—a thinker, a thinking being. This is, again, only to say something a little more fundamental about the plain facts of education. We can help ourselves to talk about metaphysics because we ourselves are metaphysical beings—physical, animal beings with rational powers that allow us to "go beyond," to transcend our surroundings in a self-conscious way. Metaphysics becomes a character of the physical, a way of being animal that we call mind. Insofar as the result of education is mind, education is the advent of metaphysics in the individual: it opens the individual up to a metaphysical life, to herself as living in a world and to all the adventurous possibilities that might entail.[19]

Conclusion

This brings us full circle to the idea that education and philosophy belong fundamentally to one another. Near the end of his lecture, Heidegger makes the following observation: "So long as man exists, philosophizing of some sort occurs. Philosophy—what we call philosophy—is metaphysics' getting under way" (1929: 110). In Chapter 1, I argued that the special connection between education and philosophy is their lack of special territory, their involvement in bringing the world in general into view. If philosophy is the activity of self-understanding as such, then it is happening in some way or other wherever there are thinking beings. If that is true, then philosophy happens profoundly in education, because education too is about how to understand ourselves and the world in which we live. Educators bring the world into view for others. They wake children to the world in the first place, teaching them how to think and how to understand themselves in relation to things in general. They do this by introducing children to language, that dynamic repository of history, the living embodiment of mind; and the effect, the fundamental achievement of education in that very broad sense, is a metaphysical transformation. It is the advent of metaphysics in the individual. It is unsurprising that "metaphysics belongs to the 'nature of man'" (109), if to be "educated" is to be metaphysical, to be able to speak and think about oneself and about reality at large—to be able to do philosophy. At the same time, to be able to do philosophy is to be able to educate in turn, to be able to help bring the world into view for others. That is indeed to say something about education that is fundamental, but not foundational: for if the result of education is the possibility of philosophy, of metaphysics' getting under way, then that means the monumental achievement of education is nothing less than the renewed possibility of education itself.

Notes

1. One notable exception is David Hume in *A Treatise of Human Nature*: "Next to the ridicule of denying an evident truth, is that of taking much pains to defend it; and no truth appears to me more evident, than that beasts are endowed with thought and reason as well as men. The arguments in this case are so obvious, that they never escape the most stupid and ignorant" (2000: I.3.xvi; 118).
2. The phrase "i.e. mind" appears in Ross's Oxford Translation (1931); in the revised translation edited by Jonathan Barnes (1984), this is replaced with "and thought." Note that rationality here is a principle—i.e., the power to act rationally—not a necessary actuality in the sense of humans acting rationally in everything they do: of course we do not! Similarly, lions are not in constant motion; and not all plants constantly take nutriment, for example when dormant in wintertime.

3   Cf., e.g., Bermudez (2006), Dretske (2006), and Glock (2000, 2009, 2010). Philosopher of mind Daniel Dennett considers the question of animal rationality in his (1995) paper "Do Animals Have Beliefs?"
4   For John McDowell, whose work I consider in the next section, the relation of language and rationality is straightforward: rationality presupposes responsiveness to reasons, and responsiveness to reasons presupposes the power to articulate and critically evaluate the grounds of one's thought and action. Only language can provide a sufficiently fine-grained articulation. This argument is well and good, but it is indifferent to the richer interrelations between language, thought and reason which I attempt to bring out in this section by drawing on the ideas of Gadamer—who influences McDowell, but perhaps not explicitly enough. In Chapter 3, I try to further appreciate the priority of language in our thinking.
5   This is partially in response to a complaint made by Amanda Baggs, an autistic blogger and activist for autists. Cf. her YouTube video "In My Language" (2007), in which she claims, "[T]he thinking of people like me is only taken seriously if we learn your language, no matter how we previously thought or interacted."
6   *Bildung* translates to education or formation, but it has far richer connotations and implications—not all of them in harmony with one another—in its long history in the German tradition. Cf., e.g., Frederick Beiser (1998) and Allen Wood (1998). Using the term without parsing its significance in that tradition would be hasty, so I generally avoid it unless, as here, it is used in passages I am citing directly.
7   Of course, by this I do not only mean formal education. The acquisition of language is a precondition of much that goes on in formal education, but at the same time formal education cultivates and enriches children's linguistic abilities and, thereby, their powers of thought.
8   "We do not learn the practice of making empirical judgments by learning rules: we are taught *judgments* and their connexion with other judgments. A *totality* of judgments is made plausible to us" (§140, original italics). "It is not single axioms that strike me as obvious, it is a system in which consequences and premises give one another *mutual* support" (§142, original italics).
9   "Admittedly, much of [McDowell's writing] is concerned with what *not* to think. But it would be wrong to deny that a positive vision emerges in this work, and if one had to say what that vision is of, 'reason's place in nature,' 'the nature of normativity' or 'the character of the space of reasons' would be appropriate answers" (102).
10 I should note that the general concept of second nature does not apply uniquely to humans for either McDowell or Bakhurst—only that the second nature that humans acquire through education is rational freedom, something that is uniquely human. Bakhurst, referring to McDowell, describes this broader sense of second nature as just "those propensities a creature acquires by 'education, habituation,

or training,' rather than as a result of 'merely biological maturation' (McDowell 2008: 220)" (Bakhurst 2011: 61; cf. also 72, n. 24). Habituation and training would be applicable to animals, whereas education would be unique to humans. On the limitations of the concept of training in the human case, cf. Rödl (2016) and Bakhurst (2014). I do not deeply value the notion of "second nature," but I do accept the view that education results in a transformation of metaphysical proportions.

11 Bakhurst notes that this metaphor can sound mechanical, but obviously the idea of being moved has a much richer sense than that. We can find ourselves "moved" by art, philosophical insight, scientific findings, the wind on the water, and hosts of other phenomena.
12 Cf. McDowell (2004: 95): "Thinking and knowing are part of our way of being animals."
13 It would not be excusable if McDowell had omitted a discussion of the significance of language altogether, but he does make "sketchy remarks" (1994: 116) at the end of his lecture. Some of those remarks appear in the passage from p. 125 quoted above.
14 I introduce Heidegger's notion of "Being" in Chapter 3.
15 This also explains the extent to which our relationship with our environment can be fatally distant, careless, and ignorant.
16 Here, Bakhurst is characterizing Rödl's point, not making an assertion of his own—even though Rödl might acquiesce in this formulation. While he is alive to Rödl's criticism, however, Bakhurst does not think "Rödl's insights wholly undermine the transformational view" (2014: 319). Cf. also Bakhurst (2016b: 124).
17 There is a philosophical literature on feral children. Cf., e.g., Candland (1993) and Malson (1972). Cf. also Harland Lane's dramatic account, *The Wild Boy of Aveyron* (1976), and the Werner Herzog's film, *The Enigma of Kaspar Hauser* (1974).
18 Cf. Wittgenstein (1993: 41).
19 Cf. Heidegger (1947: 263–4).

3

Education and History: Out into the Midst of Being

The basic aims and achievements of education are monumental, and appreciating how this is so is, in my view, a principal task of educational philosophy and of philosophy in general. This is owing to a fundamental connection between philosophy and education, namely their mutual orientation to self-understanding in relation to reality at large. As I argued in Chapter 2, this orientation is non-accidentally distinctive of humans—metaphysical beings whose power of language is tantamount to their power of rationality.

In the present chapter, I aim to appreciate further the impact of language, understood as the repository of historical mind, on the character of this orientation. First I argue that identifying language in this way ought to affect how we understand philosophical insights, in particular the idea of being at home in the world. I call attention to the insight's pedigree and suggest we attend carefully to its equivalent, the notion that we live in language. I then turn to etymology to demonstrate the priority that the thinking of our ancestors exerts, through language, over our own understanding. Etymology's overt historicity provides a good model for arriving at philosophical insights that are fundamental—not foundational—to our self-understanding. As an example I bring etymological reflection to bear on education itself. This reveals further insight into the nature of education as an event of metaphysical proportions. It also tells us more about what it means to live in language.

Ultimately the impact, through language, of history on our thinking refutes the seductive idea that our relationship to tradition is very much at our disposal. Like it or not, the insights of our dead ancestors are not themselves dead, but continue to live in language. History's living presence is part of the monumental achievement of education, whose remembrance and cultivation always await philosophy.

How Should We Develop Our Understanding of "Being at Home in the World"?

I argued in Chapter 2 that the effect of education, broadly conceived, is the advent of metaphysics in the individual insofar as she develops an orientation to the world as such by learning language. During her normal maturation, the behavior of a certain kind of animal, a human one, gradually takes on a rational character. She acquires rationality and so becomes a thinking being. Following Bakhurst and McDowell, I invoked the phrase "being at home in the world" to characterize this broad aim of education, specifically in contrast to nonhuman animals, "who are, as it were, embedded in their environment" (Gadamer 2004b: 441). The question is how to cultivate our understanding of this compelling phrase.[1]

Bakhurst, at the end of *The Formation of Reason*, calls for a "fuller account" of "what it means to be at home in the world" (2011: 161). For him, "the metaphor does not speak for itself. We need to invest it with sense" (159). He suggests that such an account, properly developed and "suitably understood," could "regulate the educational process" and "inform and inspire formal education" (161), so that "educators might draw direction or inspiration" from it (159). Yet although he offers a sketch of being at home in the world in terms of the possession of certain forms of knowledge—both theoretical and practical, and inclusive of moral knowledge and various kinds of self-knowledge (158–62; cf. 137)—Bakhurst means to leave the notion underdeveloped. He also leaves open how exactly and to what extent it can or should influence formal education.

Bakhurst's ambiguity about what a "fuller account" might look like is intentional, but two possible hazards warrant caution. Both are the result of a diminished attention to the priority of language. The first hazard is that Bakhurst appears to leave open, and even to endorse, the idea of a completed account of the aims of education, neatly assembled under the banner "Being at Home in the World." As I argued in Chapter 1, however, that sort of account is impossible. Language takes care of itself in such a way that activities like education do not require philosophical grounding. There is no such thing as a rationally justified curriculum, if that means tracing a teacher's lessons, classroom activities, and course objectives back through curriculum policy and educational theory to their conceptual or metaphysical foundations. Such foundations do not exist. Insofar as a "fuller account" of the notion of being at home in the world aspires to "regulate" education, it might as well be "prescribing and proscribing *de haut en bas*" (Blake et al. 2003: 15) education's aims and activities. In my view, that would be antithetical to one of the most valuable aspects of Bakhurst's project in *The Formation of Reason*—the delivery of insights that are fundamental to education in its centrality to human life. Such insights are fundamental in that they are broad, philosophically significant descriptions of what is already there. They do have the power greatly to "inspire" and "inform" educators and researchers interested in the actual shape of education today; but there is no final accounting for what those insights mean, because the "meaning" of anything is always open to question. As I will be arguing in Chapter 4, the question what, for us today, formal education could or should amount to is indeed of high importance, but it is also importantly perennial, that is, essentially open. It is different from, and perennial because it presupposes, the deeper question about what it means at all for education to take place—about what is most basically involved in becoming a thinking being.

It would be premature, however, to characterize Bakhurst's vision of a fuller account of being at home in the world as the mere practical systematization of those deeper insights. Even though he thinks the "issues bear on the conceptual foundations of theory and policy" and on the "educational process" itself, Bakhurst recognizes that the space of reasons and other cognate ideas are not suitable for "describing educational practice" or "characterizing pedagogical activity" (2011: 115–16). At the same time, he does not suppose it enough simply to point to the insights themselves for "reassurance" that they are philosophically significant: that "will be forthcoming only if our story about the acquisition of rationality is persuasive," and that requires "a compelling account" (152).[2] This presents another, subtler hazard.

The second hazard is more subtle because, even if an attempt at foundational thinking or practical systematization is out of the question, there can still lurk a false dichotomy between the merely "evocative image" and the "persuasive account," engendering a hierarchy of sense. It is true that the cultivation of insight involves more than therapeutic minimalism, but Bakhurst's way of putting the point can mislead. Although what it means to be at home in the world invites sustained philosophical reflection, and should be shielded from false interpretations, that is not because "the metaphor does not speak for itself" (2011: 159). On the contrary, the metaphor speaks for itself in anticipation of that reflection just as well as through it. The splendor of insight is that it speaks to us: it helps set thinking on its way; but it can only do this thanks to language's already "speculative structure" (Gadamer 2004b: 469). Language is so versatile that it presents an infinity of meaningful possibilities for exploring any situation. As the embodiment of the thinking of our ancestors it anticipates and inspires our thinking today. Language rightly enjoys "pride of place" (Bakhurst 2011: 7; McDowell 1994: 125) in the transformational view of education; but the idea it hinges on—the acquisition of language—can be construed all too narrowly, as something like obtaining readymade conceptual equipment, rather than growing into a public wellspring of untold conceptual possibilities—a "living repository of evolving forms of thought" (Bakhurst 2011: 7). We do not just inherit language: as thinkers it inheres in our thinking; it inheres in our being as thinking beings.

Being at Home in Language, Listening to Its Speech

The phrase "being at home in the world" is already historically related to the ideas taken up and developed by Bakhurst in his sociohistorical account of mind. At its heart is, appropriately and without a doubt, the centrality of language to thinking. To be at home in the world—to exist as a thinking being—is to be at home in language.

Bakhurst claims that McDowell, exploiting Gadamer and through him Heidegger and Hegel, uses the image for the "singular purpose" of contrasting human from nonhuman animals: humans live in the world; animals live in an environment (2011: 158). As I noted in Chapter 2, however, McDowell acknowledges that "Gadamer's topic … is the role of language in disclosing the world to us" (1994: 116, n. 6). For Gadamer, indeed, living in the world means living in language: "Whoever has language 'has' a world" (2004b: 449).[3] Having a world, though, is not like owning some object in the world: it is more like having a home or a location, a whereabouts in the widest sense. Having the world, we live in it. It is where we exist. Similarly, having language is not having one thing among other things: "Language is not just one of man's possessions in the world; rather, on it depends the fact that man has a *world* at all" (440; original italics). Language is basic to our having an orientation to the world as such, but then the "singular purpose" of contrasting humans and animals according to world orientation is not separable from the claim that humans live in language.

That is a clue about how to understand what it is to be at home in the world, or again, what it is to be a thinking being. We can ask what it is like to live in language; but the question already points to language itself as the primary concern. As Heidegger puts it, "Thus we are within language, at home in language, prior to everything else"—in such a way that "language itself has woven us into its speaking" (2008c: 398), and where "language speaks solely and solitarily with itself" (397). It can seem outlandish to think language is somehow the point of its own speech, but that is not far from Wittgenstein's aspiration to "recognize *how* language takes care of itself" (1961: 43; original italics). For both Heidegger and Wittgenstein, we are to understand our relationship to language as one of care or concern for what is already there. The concern is to not misread its originary significance. These formulations stress the priority of language, but it would be wrong to imagine that what they convey is only dreamy speculation in need of sober inquiry. Living in language requires careful attention to the insight as it stands. It requires hearing language when it speaks, and dwelling on what it says. "We not only *speak* language, we speak *from out of it*. We are capable of doing so only because in each case we have already listened to language. What do we hear there? We hear language speaking" (Heidegger 2008c: 411; original italics). Tautological as it may seem, thinking like this can be highly transformative.[4] I argue in Chapter 5 that philosophical reflection is at its best when it keeps such tautologies in mind: when it works at hearing the speech of insight; when it testifies to, and even embodies, language taking care of itself.

To be clear, my argument so far has not been that those philosophical accounts whose aim is clarity and persuasiveness are just barren, whereas swirls of imagery are ripe with philosophical insight. Of course not: that would simply invert the hierarchy of sense rather than relax the dichotomy it is founded on. The "ideal" of being at home in the world is, for Bakhurst, "congruent with the claim that the proper end of education is autonomy" (2011: 161). That means the phrase is just as helpful a way of understanding his account of autonomy as the reverse—and why not? Lyricism and logic can be equally insightful. Both can be obscure, and sometimes we mistake one for the other. Sometimes they explain each other.[5] The same should go for all forms of expression: we should see philosophy as that special depth of thinking available across the whole range of discourse rather than a specialized conversation with an exclusive style. The genius of language lies in its cultivating this kind of exchange.

I am suggesting the very idea of understanding something gets transformed when we begin to appreciate the impact of language on our thinking. We cannot simply do with language as we wish. Listening to the speech of language, writes Gadamer,

> requires something like a kind of heightening for the inner ear. This is obviously true for poetry and the like, but for philosophy too I take care to tell my students: you must sharpen your ear, you must realize that when you take a word in your

mouth, you have not taken up some arbitrary tool which can be thrown in a corner if it doesn't do the job, but you are committed to a line of thought that comes from afar and reaches on beyond you.

(2004a: 551–2)

For the idea of being at home in the world, this is especially true: it already enjoys an historical connection with much important philosophy of the previous century; it also asks something fundamental about the self-understanding of humanity, and is therefore central to philosophical reflection. The point, though, is not just that respect for language's historicity will be relevant to our understanding that idea in particular. Rather, in paying attention to the priority of language in our reflections, the whole historical dimension of language emerges in its monumental complexity and locates us somewhere deep within its folds. That is a general statement about understanding as it relates to its own historicity—the main theme of this chapter—but etymology offers more concrete examples of this phenomenon.

Etymology and the Temporal Nature of Language

Etymology is the study of words in light of their historical development: it looks at a word's origins and the way in which its form and meaning have changed over time. Like any historical inquiry it deploys a variety of methods, but in particular etymology examines vocabularies and texts from languages young and old. Unsurprisingly there are whole families of modern derivatives in many languages of the same ancient word form, whose histories have been affected by migration, war, and other sorts of political upheaval, as well as artistic, intellectual, and technological achievement—the ebb and flow of cultural transformation. Such historical complexities are coextensive with the life stories of individual people.

Applied to itself, the word "etymology" derives from Greek *etymon* (true sense) and the suffix *logia* (study of); so etymology self-identifies as the study of the true sense of words. How "true sense" should be understood, though, is of particular interest here. It shows us how we can recognize philosophical insights as fundamental but not foundational—a demonstration promised in Chapter 2. The key to this is the historicity of language.

It is important that, for etymology, the idea of arriving at some absolutely true sense of a word is out of the question. It is not even clear what that could mean. If a word's true sense were just its ancient form, etymology would be more like the study of meaning's dissolution over time rather than its cultivation. Etymology might then be considered at once the highest form of intellectual inquiry and the least interesting: the former because of a perceived need to return to some original, perfectly meaningful and true language; the latter because of its utter hopelessness.

It would be hopeless, for one, because of the impossibility of deciding "where" language "began" over the course of human development. That is an idea whose incoherence we find in the gradual acquisition of language in children, as well as in the good sense of describing some animal behaviors as proto-linguistic.[6] Nowhere could we find an original language spoken by permanently prehistoric beings; nor could we find some single utterance that somehow captures all of the "meaning" of everything else spoken throughout history. As Gadamer observes, the first would be the "language of Adam" and the second would be the "ineffable Word of God … reflected in everything" (2004b: 435–6).[7] Both would be essentially ahistorical: one totally static, the other outside time.[8]

Meanwhile the versatility of meaning that is the lifeblood of language is nothing apart from its temporal existence. Language is the behavior of a particular kind of being, a rational one, who lives in time and knows itself to do so. In language we judge one thing on the basis of another and "carry over" meaning from here to there, then to now. This "living metaphoricity" permits an untold array of possibilities for future expression, facilitating the intellectual freedom and creativity we constantly enjoy.[9] The life of a language, moreover, is so intertwined with the history of its speakers that the sense of one cannot be seriously considered without a sense for the other. Culture is not separable from language. We could not describe world history to our satisfaction using only Sumerian forms of speech, for example.[10]

The chronological inverse of that primitivistic approach to etymology would be for a dictionary to claim to have registered the "absolute true sense" of words, as though some one modern language had finally attained "crystalline purity" (Wittgenstein 1958: §108). We know from previous discussion that that idea is equally hopeless. Language has no more a final form than a beginning. To imagine the end of its incessant proliferation of variety and possibility might be to imagine a kind of saturation point of meaning, but not only does that contradict our normal experience, where simply being in a situation presents a host of possibilities for thought, speech, and action. It also ignores the fact that the rush of time unceasingly rearranges the contextual present, offering new insight into the past. "Historical tradition can be understood only as something always in the process of being defined by the course of events" (Gadamer 2004b: 366). Every artifact, expression, situation, or event—a war, a tooth, an inscription, anything, from however long ago—supports a range of applicable interpretations and explanations whose scope only increases as times change.

It is no surprise that dictionaries register current language conventions in a way that does little more than convey a general standard for the here and now. They only offer a contemporary profile of an essentially historical phenomenon—the linguistic behavior of rationally free beings living in a particular time. Not even literal definitions are exempt from historical development. Those are just ports of entry into all the varieties of meaningful thought and expression that a word can possibly sustain, "literal" or not. Every event of language is an invitation to all sorts of new variety insofar as it provokes interpretation, reaction, and explication.

> Thus every word, as the event of a moment, carries with it the unsaid, to which it is related by responding and summoning. The occasionality of human speech is not a casual imperfection of its expressive power; it is, rather, the logical expression of the living virtuality of speech that brings a totality of meaning into play, without being able to express it totally. All human speaking is finite in such a way that there is laid up within it an infinity of meaning to be explicated and laid out.
>
> (Gadamer 2004b: 454)

The intellectual freedom that language supports is a temporal freedom through and through. Language is always the "event of a moment," wherein something comes to presence out of the past and in anticipation of the future. Its explication is never complete. "[T]here can be no doubt that the great horizon of the past, out of which our culture and our present live, influences us in everything we want, hope for, or fear in the future. History is only present to us in light of our futurity" (Gadamer 1966b: 9).

Etymology's "True Sense": A Model for Philosophical Insight

What does etymology study when it studies the "true sense" of words, if "absolute meaning" is already out of the question? The same consideration that precludes absolute sense in etymological inquiry—the historical dimension of language and hence of the inquiry itself—characterizes the "true sense" of etymology as follows. By studying the historical roots of a word, etymology discovers a fundamental unity of meaning in which the roots' subsequent variations participate, where the sheer variety of those derivations reveals their coherence exactly as derivatives of something. That presupposed "something" is the "true sense" of which etymology is in pursuit, but as a unity it is only achievable in light of its historicity, so it cannot be called foundational in any robust sense.

Put a slightly different way, etymology arrives at the true sense of a word by locating it in the historical context of language, orienting the word to its own history. The word's true sense, though, is not locatable anywhere in particular in that history, because it just is the location of the word itself: it is the approximate totality of relations and family resemblances that situate the word as one of a whole variety of manifestations of its originary form. The totality is approximate, because its history is not done, and nor does it have a clear beginning; but that is exactly the sense in which the unity of meaning achieved through etymological inquiry can be understood as both fundamental and not foundational. The unity depends on the open-endedness of its subject matter and does not aspire to some absolute form.

The "true sense" of etymological understanding is not static. It is a coherent variety always under development, in accordance with the thinking of normal people as they go about their normal lives. That is the source of its philosophical significance. Although a unity of meaning emerges through it, within that unity awaits a renewed appreciation for further possibilities for creative expression and thought. Etymology is philosophically valuable, not as plain historical inquiry, but in its delivery of insight and of advance conceptual support for meaningful variations on that same unity. It does not preemptively block those variations. It anticipates and inspires and thereby stays true to the idea of language as a living repository of historical tradition, a fountain of possibilities for thinking.

Heidegger writes in "On the Way to Language," "On what does the essence of language rest; in what is it grounded? Perhaps when we search for grounds we pass on by the essence of language" (2008c: 412). This is reminiscent of Wittgenstein's metaphor of doing philosophy as something like discovering the foundations of one's convictions, which, however, turn out to be carried by the whole house (1972: §248). I adopted that metaphor in Chapter 1 to describe how language takes care of itself, but also in Chapter 2 as a way to understand how philosophy can still arrive at deeper insights about things without pretending to foundationalism. The structure applies just as well to etymology. The true sense of a word is just the way the word harkens back to its own historical roots and coheres with other manifestations of the same. Etymology unifies the variety of those manifestations and opens the way for more. Similarly, philosophical insight can reveal the conceptual unity of a family of ideas and practices without pretending to have discovered any conceptual or metaphysical foundations. Such insight inspires more philosophical reflection and more variety. What it unifies is a host of "evolving forms of thought" (Bakhurst 2011: 7) and ultimately of human life.

Education as a Leading Out and a Leading In

So far I have been trying to get a sense of the impact of language, as the repository of historical tradition, on our thinking and hence on the nature of education. I began by arguing that the notion of being at home in the world as a fundamental educational achievement does not need to be processed by sober theory to register its insightfulness. We should rather allow ourselves to heed the insight's historical and conceptual equivalent, our living in language. A step in that direction is to ask how language anticipates our own understanding, of which etymology's explicit historicity offers a good example.

I have just finished suggesting that etymology also reveals a way of understanding philosophical insight. Philosophy can ask after the true sense of things, where that is understood as analogous to the historically oriented "true sense" of words pursued by etymology—a diversified conceptual unity that is also a living source of creative reflection. The idea is for philosophy to be able to locate and explore common conceptual denominators and so point the way to a better and more profound understanding of things. "Thinking attends to these simple relationships. It tries to find the right word for them within the long-traditional language and grammar of metaphysics" (Heidegger 1947: 237). We can demonstrate this by applying etymological reflection to concepts relevant to education itself. That in turn will shed light on the notion of living in language and thus on what it means to be at home in the world.

The Latin root of "education" is *educare* (to lead forth), which derives from *ducere* (to lead) and the prefix *ex* (out); so education identifies etymologically as some kind of leading out. Recall that near the end of Chapter 2 I described education as effecting the advent of metaphysics for the individual. I adopted Heidegger's conception of metaphysics as "being beyond beings"—or what comes to the same, "being held out into the nothing" or "being in the world." To be minded is to enjoy a metaphysical existence by having an orientation to reality at large; it is to be able to transcend one's environment by thinking "beings as a whole."[11]

This is in harmony with the etymological point Heidegger makes about the word "metaphysics." The Greek phrase *(ta) meta (ta) physika* ([the work] after [the] physics, beyond physics) was originally used to catalogue a work of Aristotle's on the common structures of things. So named because it was listed after a work entitled *Physics*, some scholars nevertheless interpreted *Metaphysics* as the name of an inquiry into what is beyond the physical—a fitting interpretation given the subject matter of Aristotle's text.[12] For Heidegger, Dasein or "being in the world" is "metaphysical" exactly in the sense of its "being beyond beings" and so having the capacity to understand things in general. It is a distinctively human mode of existence, where the very existence of things is a possible subject of inquiry. Humans exist in a way that no other creatures do, because we recognize the existence of things as such—as things existing.[13]

The idea that the world exists for humans in a unique way resonates strikingly with Heidegger's conception of the metaphysical if we consider the etymology, frequently exploited by Heidegger, of the word "existence."[14] It derives from the Latin *existere* (to stand forth, to be), from *sistere* (to take a stand) and prefix *ex* (out, out from within).[15] According to this conceptual constellation, the world "stands out" for us as for no other creature, and this means our own existence is of a special sort: we stand out among other beings, as beings who recognize the world's existence as such, as standing out. More than that, if education gives us an orientation to reality at large, it gives us a sense both of the existence of the world and of our own existence. The metaphysical effect then is not just that we come to stand out among other beings in the sense of becoming rational—"a *metaphysical* difference" (McDowell 2009b: 172; original italics)—but that we as individuals come to stand out before the world in general in recognizing ourselves as individuals who live in the world. We recognize ourselves individually as standing out beyond beings as a whole.[16] That is a way to understand the etymological significance of education as a leading out. Through education we are led out into existence in general, where the world as world stands out for us, and where we stand out to ourselves as being in the world.

Now insofar as education is the broad realization of our self-conscious existence, we can say it introduces us to ourselves as metaphysical beings. Education is indeed "the child's growth into itself" (2016: 87).[17] The etymology of "introduce" is conspicuously related to that of education. They share a Latin root. The word *introducere* (to bring in, to lead in) derives from *ducere* (to lead), as *educare* does; but its prefix is *intro* (inward). If education is a leading out into the world as something that stands out for us, it is also a leading inward to ourselves as beings who stand out in the world just by recognizing ourselves as being in the world. Accordingly, through education we are at once introduced to the world and to ourselves: we are led out and into the world and hence into ourselves as standing out beyond beings.

Recognizing ourselves and the world as standing out in relation to one another requires language, the medium of understanding. Our acquiring it is the way in which we become educated. "[L]anguage is a medium where I and world meet or, rather, manifest their original belonging together" (2004b: 469). The idea that language prepares the setting for the mutual standing out of world and self is fundamental to understanding. It relates to one of Heidegger's most famous statements about language: "Language is the house of Being. In its home man dwells" (1947: 217). This takes some explication.

Language as the House of Being

Heidegger's lifelong task was to make explicit the question of the meaning of Being—the unifying principle of existence, universality as such, what he calls "*the transcendens pure and simple*" (1927: 85; original italics and stylization). It was, arguably, the original question of the ancient Greek pre-Socratic philosophers, especially Parmenides and Heraclitus. Although it appears somewhat in the works of Plato and Aristotle, Heidegger's main criticism of the ensuing metaphysical tradition of Western philosophy and its modern techno-scientific disposition is that it has been plagued by a forgetfulness of that very question; but the question makes metaphysics itself a possible line of inquiry, along with natural science.[18] Both endeavors have been involved in the study of "beings"— that is, of things—but not of the "Being of beings"—a concept presupposed by any study of what is.

For Heidegger, the question of the meaning of Being has historically been concealed as a result of three related prejudices. First, "Being" is universal: it appears everywhere, in every assertion or thought about anything, so it does not as a self-standing concept obviously present some further issue for discussion. Second, "Being" is impossible to define in a non-circular way: it is so immediate that it cannot but appear in its own definition. Third, "Being" is self-evident: when it appears in some statement, such as "The sky is blue" or "I am happy," everyone already understands what is being said and no further clarification is necessary.[19] The sum of these prejudices is that Being as such is not very problematic or thought provoking. Heidegger disagrees with that conclusion, however: "The fact that we live already in an understanding of Being and that the meaning of Being is at the same time shrouded in darkness proves the fundamental necessity of recovering the question of the meaning of 'Being'" (1927: 44). Because we are the sorts of beings for whom our own existing in the world faces us as a question; because that question, even when we fail to face it, defines our mode of being; and because our understanding of the very idea of existence and its unifying concept—Being, at all—is everywhere, but everywhere only partial; the basic question of the meaning of Being should, above all, be made explicit.

> Yet Being—what is Being? It is It itself. The thinking that is to come must learn to experience that and to say it. "Being"—that is not God and not a cosmic ground. Being is farther than all beings and is yet nearer to man than every being, be it a rock, a beast, a work of art, a machine, be it an angel or God. Being is the nearest. Yet the near remains farthest from man.
>
> (1947: 234)

For Heidegger, especially in his early and most influential work, *Being and Time*, recovering and clarifying the question of the meaning of Being requires an "'historical' interpretation" of that "historic" being for whom its own existence is a question—Dasein, "being in the world" as such (1927: 86–7).[20] The temporality of Dasein would remain central both to his critique of Western metaphysics and to his task of making the question of Being explicit. In his later writings, however, Heidegger would place more emphasis on the historicity of language itself, especially poetic language, as the setting of the "essential unfolding" of the Being of beings and, especially, of the Being of Dasein.[21] This slight shift in emphasis usually referred to in German as the *"Kehre"* (turn) reflects dissatisfaction with his initial aim of clarifying the question of Being. That aim was still shaped by the language and grammar of the Western metaphysical tradition, which "questions what is present only with regard to its presence" (1972: 446). He therefore began around 1930 to pay more attention to language as that which, unfolding in time, brings to unconcealment, or presence, what was once concealed and might be concealed again.[22] "Language," he writes, "is the clearing-concealing advent of Being itself" (1947: 230). The temporality of language means it both clears and conceals, folding and unfolding historically as things are brought to language, explained, misunderstood, known, reinterpreted, remembered, and so on. Language is alive in history. If we attend to the way in which we "bring to language" as a temporal act, then we are attending to "something of the essential unfolding of Being itself" (263). That reflects the way we "dwell" in the "house of Being": as historical beings we live in language, where we tend to Being's unfolding.

Standing in the Midst of Being

Acquiescing in talk of language unfolding Being may sound as though we are uncritically being swept into obscurantism, but let us again pay attention to the insight as it stands and try to hear what it says. Language "unfolds" by making explicit. The word "explicit" derives from the Latin *explicare* (to unfold), from *plicare* (to fold) and prefix *ex* (out): according to this etymological arrangement, in being made explicit things unfold, folding out in language. What unfolds in a word is not just an idea that gets spoken out or written down. The things themselves—the events, stories, situations, histories, the world in general—unfold temporally in language and are brought to our attention as objects of the understanding.[23] The folding out of the world in language corresponds to the idea that language prepares a place, a conceptual space where things stand out in relation to one another. By bringing things to explicit language rational beings can achieve conceptual distance and see things for what they are. In education we are introduced to this conceptual space—the space of reasons—where the world gradually unfolds before us and things begin to stand out to us, exciting our attention.

That is a genuinely metaphysical effect of education; and the effect is essentially historical, owing to the historicity of language itself. As the house of Being, language does not stand outside existence. It is what brings existence as such to conceptual possibility. As an unfolding, whatever clarity we achieve through explicit language is not that of "a standpoint that is beyond any standpoint" (Gadamer 2004b: 369), outside of time and space, where everything is suddenly made perfectly transparent to us—"as though being human exempted one from having to be somewhere in particular" (McDowell 1994: 118). No such standpoint exists. On the contrary, the historicity of language means we achieve clarity by standing out in the clearing of Being, where we have a view of things from the standpoint of our own historical situation; but that situation is finite, and many things remain concealed from us; but only because of the concealment of things can things become unconcealed. The historicity of language means the metaphysical effect of education is temporal through and through. Being held out into the nothing and beyond beings as a whole we are likewise not held out into nonbeing: rather we are held out into that space prepared by language that allows us to understand at all. Education is not only a leading out: it is also a leading in.

This brings us finally to a fresh view of that out and into which education leads. In language things are brought to the clearing of Being. There they stand out. We too are at first led out and into this clearing through education, so that we stand out in relation to the world. One of Gadamer's most superb formulations in *Truth and Method* is this: "*Being that can be understood is language*" (2004: 470; original italics). That is no immediate surprise: in language we understand; it is the medium of our understanding, the house of Being in which we dwell. The word "understanding," however—and it is the direct translation of Gadamer's German *verstanden*—derives from Old English *understandan* (to stand in the midst of), from *standan* (to stand) and prefix *under* (beneath, among, before, in the presence of).[24] Gadamer's statement then can be reworded: Being that can be stood-in-the-midst-of is language.

Here we find a way to understand education's "true sense" as a leading out into the midst of Being. Through education we partake of the "transcendens" of Being by transcending our environment and coming to stand out in relation to existence in general. This happens in language, the house of Being: dwelling in its house, we stand in its midst. As metaphysical beings who live in language we are held out into the nothing, beyond beings, and that means we have been led out and into the midst of universality as such. Having attended a little more closely to language's unfolding, however, we can also see that this metaphysical standpoint does not only involve our understanding of things in the here and now. Rather the historical dimension of language shows itself to be fundamental to our being at home in the world. Language, the house of Being, is the repository of historical mind, the living embodiment of the thinking of our ancestors. Attending to its historicity, we find ourselves located somewhere in a whole living tradition of humans coming to stand in the midst of Being—the history of mind itself, taking care of itself, gathering itself into itself like the soul of Socrates in his preparation for death.[25] What is monumental about education is our bearing witness to and partaking in that.

Conclusion: The Rortian Alternative

In this chapter, I have argued for the significance of the historicity of language in our understanding of education, and especially of its metaphysical effect. This has led to several related insights about our living in language and what it means to be at home in the world, to be a thinking being. I believe those insights remain true to themselves in that they anticipate creative reflection and criticism and do not aspire to some absolute arrangement or foundational status.

I conclude as I began, by contrasting a diminished attention to the priority of language, but now from a slightly different direction. My focus here is an attitude that calls itself "historicist" but in my view is really not. It is Richard Rorty's American pragmatism. Proponents of his philosophy might imagine that the idea of being at home in the world does not speak for itself very much at all, or that what it says is for us to decide, based on the practical issues facing us today in education, politics, or any relevant discourse. To imagine this, though, would be to fall into the subtler hazard, mentioned near the beginning of this chapter, of ignoring the living historicity of language by drawing a hierarchy of sense between the merely evocative metaphor and the literal account.

Rorty is not subtle about drawing this hierarchy, however. He supports it explicitly when he describes his view of the historical nature of language. For him, language is just a mechanism for helping us cope with the world, and the point of intellectual discourse is to refine language for the sake of public coping. Discourse accomplishes this task by working at "literalizing" the metaphoric character of a particular insight such that it becomes a kind of truism, a bit of unquestionable meaning, in some language or vocabulary. Rorty's view of the process is essentially that it is assisted suicide for metaphors. "Old metaphors," he writes, "are constantly dying off into literalness, and then serving as a platform and foil for new metaphors" (1989c: 16). The purpose of normal intellectual discourse then is to

> assimilate, by gradually literalizing, the new metaphors which [a "great" or "abnormal"][26] thinker has provided. The proper honor to pay new, vibrantly alive metaphors, is to help them become dead metaphors as quickly as possible, to rapidly reduce them to the status of tools for social progress. The glory of the philosopher's thought is not that it initially makes everything more difficult, (though that is, of course, true) but that in the end it makes things easier for everybody.
>
> (1991c: 17)

In Rorty's view, most of the metaphors of historical discourse, especially those that come up again and again in the received philosophical canon, have been paid their full tribute many times over. They now hinder social progress because they are taken too seriously as somehow "reflecting reality as it really is," beyond language—a metaphor in itself. The result is that new, more useful metaphors are not taken seriously enough. His seminal work, *Philosophy and the Mirror of Nature*, is an attempt to criticize and move beyond a particular group of metaphors that has haunted philosophy at least since Descartes. Rorty's pragmatism consists in arguing that, so long as we continue to impose those old, dead metaphors on today's discourse, they will only hinder our creativity and our ability to find solutions to the practical issues facing us today. Our retaining them is only about satisfying "a disposition to use the language of our ancestors" and therefore "to worship the corpses of their metaphors" (1989c: 21).

Rorty calls his view historicist because it is based on the idea that the so-called perennial problems of traditional philosophy are merely historically contingent, and are therefore not perennial at all. He tries to downplay their perceived universal grandeur by pointing to their historical development, suggesting they are really questions about style, method, and vocabulary— what he calls "'conceptual' metaissues thrown off by the special disciplines or more generally by other areas of culture," but not, as philosophy has apparently claimed, "always about the same topics" (1984: 263). This means broad categories like "truth," "nature," "reality," and "Being" are simply "God surrogates" (261), invented language born out of a desire to "escape from history" (1979: 9) and become a "spectator of time and eternity" (1991d: 51). Rather than try to converge on some ahistorical truth as envisioned by our ancestors, Rorty believes we should "bring humanity to full maturity by discarding the image of the fierce father figure" (1998a: 151–2) and "overcome the tyranny of the past over the future" (2007a: 85). We have, he believes, reached a point in history where it has become impossible to "pour new wine into old wine bottles, and write in a way which is continuous with the philosophical tradition" (1988: 161), because there is no such tradition, if that means an essential narrative of Western metaphysics. His historicism is meant to teach us that philosophical problems are not found, but made—even that we should think of "truth as made rather than found" (1989c: 3). He urges us to feel empowered by this knowledge and to work to overcome tradition by means of radical self-creation. "The pragmatist thus exalts spontaneity at the cost of receptivity, as his realist opponent did the reverse" (1985: 89).

For all Rorty's attention to the historicity of language, however, his view is streaked with a kind of anti-historicism, what Gadamer might have called "historical alienation."[27] It is true, as McDowell puts it, that "tradition is subject to reflective modification by each generation that inherits it," and even that "a standing obligation to engage in critical reflection is itself part of the inheritance" (1994: 126). It would be wrong to conclude from this, however, that there is a possibility of criticizing that language and tradition from sideways on. For a person to be able to do any criticizing, "the first thing that needs to happen is for her to be initiated into a tradition as it stands" (126). Any reflection we engage in is already situated within a tradition. Of course this does not preclude criticism, for ours is a tradition of critical reflection and calls us to engage with it as that. For us, part of being initiated into tradition is being critical of it.

Rorty thinks we need to emancipate ourselves from the clutches of history, because some of its discourse has involved a failed search for objectivity—"reality as it really is" outside the bounds of language. He is right about the failure of that notion and about our need to get beyond it by exploring new ways of thinking, but the idea of emancipation from tradition as such constitutes a faulty objectivity of its own. Gadamer urges us rather to

> see through the dogmatism of asserting an opposition and separation between the ongoing, natural "tradition" and the reflective appropriation of it. For behind this assertion stands the dogmatic objectivism … [in which] the understander is seen … in such a way as to imply that his own understanding does not enter into the event.
>
> (Gadamer 1967b: 28)

There is no emancipating ourselves from tradition because our critically reflecting on it remains entirely within its purview—not that we need emancipating in the first place. We are "emancipated" precisely through our initiation into tradition and our achievement of the intellectual freedom to engage with it reflectively and learn from its successes and failures. We cannot simply lay it to waste because we feel we have been misled by it. The "assertion that reason and authority are abstract antitheses" is unacceptable: "In it, reflection is granted a false power" (33). In order to reach "maturity" we do not kill our elders or try to destroy their memory when they are dead. Maturity is about understanding the wisdom and strength of those who have gone before—despite, even in light of, their blunders and brutalities—in a comprehensive attempt to become better than what they have been, what we have been. I do not "discard the image of the fierce father figure" by killing my father. I realize that he was and remains a child of history, as I am and remain his child. He too is an understander, as I am, and as my child is. Together we are part of a long tradition of understanding and being misunderstood, misunderstanding and being understood. Tradition is much "more than a mere object of our free acceptance or rejection" (1966b: 4).

"For language is not only an object in our hands, it is the reservoir of tradition and the medium in and through which we exist and perceive our world" (Gadamer 1967b: 29). Language is the wellspring of thought—the origin of critical thinking, not its nadir. Thinking in language means we already live in its midst. As I hope to have shown in the foregoing, our relationship with historical tradition is far from some mere contrast of the living to the dead, or of the urgent present to the distant past. It is a living relationship characterized by the sheer presence of history in the everyday—right here in our own language. We can see this by attending to the historical life of the words we speak. Their history speaks from out of the past, not only to you and me but also to the children of the future far beyond us. In speaking these words we harken back to the speech of our ancestors and so partake in their thinking, just as we anticipate and partake in the thinking of those yet to come. Etymology makes this living historical relationship explicit by revealing the still vibrant metaphoric life of our apparently literal language.

Similarly, philosophy need not be seen as some perennial attempt of intellectual discourse to stand outside its own historicity. As explicit understanding it stands, and always attempts to stand, exactly within it, and that is the source of its perenniality. When doing philosophy we try to get a true sense of things, such as education, or of how things in general hang together. We are not trying to get beyond language—just the reverse! We are trying to locate ourselves exactly in the world, in the incomplete whole of language, the history of human life, and the radical questionability of the universe. Having been introduced to ourselves through education as thinking beings, we are simply trying to come to terms with reality and thereby to understand ourselves—to locate ourselves and find ourselves where we already are, standing in the midst of ourselves—standing in the midst of Being.

Notes

1   Again I am posing philosophical approach as a question. This is not a "metaphilosophical" discussion, however. Thinking that would wrongly assume that philosophy is method, and that talking about the character of philosophy is therefore not philosophy but something else—something "more meta." In my view, philosophy is "meta" through and through: it is self-understanding as such. "One might think: if philosophy speaks of the use of the word 'philosophy' there must be a second-order philosophy. But it is not so: it is, rather, like the case of orthography, which deals with the word 'orthography' among others without then being second-order" (Wittgenstein 1958: §121). This may seem in tension with Heidegger—especially the later Heidegger—who often uses "philosophy" and "metaphysics" interchangeably to denote the traditional Western pursuit and its language, grammar, style, and assumptions, in place of which he promotes a less formal but more "rigorous" kind of thinking (cf. Heidegger 1972). I do not think there is

any real tension, however, as I hope the ensuing discussion will show. Gadamer's "Heidegger and the Language of Metaphysics" (1967a) touches on this issue.
2   Bakhurst contrasts his own approach with McDowell's "Wittgensteinian aversion to constructive philosophizing," specifically about the notion of *Bildung* (Bakhurst 2011: 152). He discusses McDowell's "thin teleology" in Chapter 1 (2011: 8–10).
3   "Not only is the world world only insofar as it comes into language, but language, too, has its real being only in the fact that the world is presented in it" (440).
4   Cf. Paul Fairfield's (2016) "A Phenomenology of Listening."
5   Take as an example the epigraph at the beginning of Gadamer's *Truth and Method* (2004b: v).
6   Notice that this is neither a strictly empirical observation, nor an observation about the limits of our scientific powers, nor a bald endorsement of the so-called Recapitulation Thesis, i.e., the view that the normal biological development of a member of a species recapitulates the stages of the evolution of the species itself. This is, rather, a conceptual point about the incoherence of the idea that the "origin" of language anywhere is an all-or-nothing matter. It does vaguely resemble the Recapitulation Thesis, but not as a biological theory or empirical hypothesis: it simply makes sense of both the gradual evolution of our species and the gradual development of language in the human individual, while also making conceptual room for talking coherently but modestly about nonhuman animal cognition, as in Chapter 2 above.
7   Cf. Gadamer (1966a: 60–1, 63): "An important advance occurred when the answer to the question of the origin of language was sought in the nature of man instead of in the biblical story of creation. For then a further step was unavoidable: the naturalness of language made it impossible to inquire any longer about an original condition in which man was without language. With this the very question of the origin of language was excluded altogether. … What sort of folly is it to say that a child speaks a 'first' word. What kind of madness is it to want to discover the original language of humanity by having children grow up in hermetic isolation from human speaking and then, from their first babbling of an articulate sort, recognize an actual human language and accord it the honor of being the 'original' language of creation. What is mad about such ideas is that they want to suspend in some artificial way our very enclosedness in the linguistic world in which we live. In truth we are always already at home in language, just as much as we are in the world."
8   Cf. Gadamer (2004b: 418–26).
9   Cf. Gadamer (2004b: 432–6).
10 This can seem either trivially true or patently false, but it is neither. It is a way of saying that a discourse can only be understood, as it were, from the inside: not just them understanding something foreign requires adopting a perspective different from but still resembling one's own, but that that is what happens anyway in the

study of other languages, cultures, and histories. Cf. Donald Davidson (1986) on radical interpretation and the principle of charity. This idea of moving from one standpoint to another—a sort of "fusion of horizons" (cf. Gadamer 2004b: 302–6, 386–91; Bakhurst 2011: 96, n. 20)—corresponds to my suggestion in Chapter 2 above that language is importantly versatile: it is both stable and supple enough to allow for new ways of understanding and applying concepts. Another way of putting this is to say with Gadamer that language, like knowledge, "admits of a more and a less" (2004b: 435).

The point also relates to the gist of a famous collection of passages in Wittgenstein (1958: §§243–309) sometimes referred to as the Private Language Argument. In it, Wittgenstein argues that no one could create a language that refers only to her own "inner sensations," since there would be no possibility for recognizing error in usage. The connection here is this: it is not impossible for someone to make up a language—take as an example Valarin, an angelic tongue from J. R. R. Tolkien's *Lord of the Rings* legendarium (Tolkien 1999)—but artificial languages already borrow from and incorporate the meaningfulness of the language normally spoken by their creators, where that language is always already both public and historical in nature. A logically independent language is not even artificial: it is no language at all; equally, no language is totally independent from all others. That is why there is no such thing as a totally dead language, since if it is a language, even existing only as ancient text, it is already understood in some way or other as such; so its structure, significance, and conceptual relations to the world and to other languages are already interesting, meaningful questions. The Rosetta Stone, on display at the British Museum in London, England, since the beginning of the nineteenth century, is a good example of this.

11   Cf. Heidegger's (1929) "What Is Metaphysics?"
12   Cf. Heidegger (1929: 106). This general narrative about the history of the word "metaphysics" is widely accepted. Cf. Ross (1924: xxxii) and Cohen (2015).
13   "The world as world exists for man as for no other creature that is in the world" (Gadamer 2004b: 440; cited in Chapter 2).
14   Cf. Heidegger (1947: 228–34; 1927: 54–7; and 2008b: 126–7).
15   This is also true of the German equivalent, *existenz*. "Heidegger coins the term *existentiell* (here translated as 'existentiell') to designate the way Dasein in any given case actually exists by realizing or ignoring its various possibilities—in other words, by living its life. *One* of these possibilities is to inquire into the *structure* of its life and possibilities; the kind of understanding thereby gained Heidegger calls *existenzial* (here translated as 'existential'). The nexus of such structures he call [sic] *Existentialität* (here translated as 'existentiality')" (editor David Ferrell Krell in Heidegger 1927: 55, n.; original italics).
16   This is in harmony with Heidegger's (1947: 226–34), McDowell's (1994: 63–5), and Bakhurst's (2011: 127) rejection of the idea that humans are "rational animals" only

in the sense of having an animal core plus having something extra: rationality. In fact, our rationality permeates our being from the inside out, in a way that does not just make us special among other beings but totally reorients our mode of life. As rational beings we are oriented fundamentally to reality at large and hence to our own existence.

17 This phrase is cited in Chapter 2. Rödl attributes it to Aristotle but does not provide a reference.

18 Cf. the Introduction to *Being and Time*, Chapter 1, e.g., "Dasein is a being that does not simply occur among other beings. Rather it is ontically distinguished by the fact that in its Being this being is concerned *about* its very Being. … *Understanding of Being is itself a determination of the Being of Dasein*" (1927: 54; original italics).

19 Cf. Heidegger (1927: 42–3).

20 Cf. Heidegger (1927: 60–4; 1947: 239).

21 The phrase "essential unfolding" appears, e.g., in Heidegger (1929: 104; and 1947: 263, cited below).

22 This is a decisive theme in Heidegger. The idea of an historical movement from concealment to unconcealment forms the basis of Heidegger's critique of Western metaphysics, "which questions what is present only with regard to its presence" (1972: 446). Heidegger explicitly rejects the idea of "presence" as mere ahistorical "truth" and explores of the idea of "truth" as inherently also "untruth" or "concealment": "Or does [our lack of understanding of *alētheia*] happen because self-concealing, concealment, *lēthē*, belongs to *a-lētheia*, not as mere addition, not as shadow to light, but rather as the heart of *alētheia*?" (448). Both his critique of the metaphysical tradition and his exploration of "concealment" and "unconcealment" were deeply influenced by Friedrich Nietzsche (cf. esp. 1873). They also had a major influence on Jacques Derrida, whose famous concept of "deconstruction"—the critical analysis of conceptual systems that conceal their own historicity and rhetorical devices—owes much to Heidegger's notion of the "*Destruktion*" of tradition. Neither "*Destruktion*" nor "deconstruction," however, is anything like a flat rejection of historical tradition. In fact, in the translation of the Introduction to *Being and Time*, the word "*Destruktion*" is rendered "destructuring" to reflect this (cf. 1927: 63, n.). I make a similar point in my criticism of Richard Rorty on our relationship to historical tradition in the concluding section of this chapter.

23 Cf. Gadamer (2004b: 425): "[F]or the word is not expressing the mind but the thing intended. The starting point for the formation of the word is the substantive content … that fills the mind. The thought seeking expression refers not to the mind but to the thing."

24 The English, German, Sanskrit, Latin, Greek, and other cognates derive from Proto-Indo-European *nter- (between, among).

25 Cf. Plato's *Phaedo* (1966: §21 [67a–d]). In this passage Socrates is discussing the purification of the soul through philosophy, apparently by rejection of the physical world. I think we can maintain the image of mind gathering itself into itself without acquiescing in any dualism of that sort.
26 From the same page: "The pragmatist would grant Heidegger's point that the great thinkers are the most idiosyncratic." In *Philosophy and the Mirror of Nature*, Rorty describes "abnormal discourse" as "what happens when someone joins in the discourse who is ignorant of [its] conventions or who sets them aside" (1979: 320).
27 Cf. Gadamer (1967b; 2004b: Chapter 3 [B]).

4

The Structure of Educational Ideals: Transcendental Origins, Impossible Aims

I have been trying to articulate an educational philosophy where the aims and achievements of education are of monumental, metaphysical proportions, and where education and philosophy belong profoundly to one another. The approach has been to say things that are fundamental about education, but not foundational to its endeavors, in hopes that our thinking about it might be transformed from the inside out. In particular I have argued that education in the broadest sense effects a metaphysical transformation in the individual, such that the world as world comes to stand out for her. That is thanks to her learning language, the repository of historical mind. Through education a child becomes a thinking being and thereby locates herself in the universe as such: she is led out into reality at large—held out into the nothing—introduced to herself as someone who dwells in the midst of Being. Now this kind of thinking can seem as trivial as it is profound: it can seem to ignore a more concrete discourse surrounding education, about what it might be aiming at in a richer sense. I address that issue in the present chapter.

A longstanding question is just how substantial a conception of the educated person, or of the aims of education, is appropriate. My intention is not to answer this question head-on, but to alter its shape by recognizing a duality in the very idea of an educational aim. Failure to appreciate this duality can confound discussion by conflating the real, fundamental achievements of education with the essential ideality of its ideals. The result is that the question of aims in education appears reduced to a question either of merely local norms, which can seem presumptuous and stifling, or else of indeterminate universals, which can seem vague and impractical. My suggestion is this. To recognize a fundamental achievement of education, such as rational freedom, is to point to an ideal whose possibilities of realization remain essentially open. The aim is entirely authentic because it is basic to our understanding of human being, at all; but its maximal achievement remains practically and conceptually unavailable, owing at once to the aim's abstract ideality and to its entanglement with other basic aims. Enriching our understanding of an educational ideal is therefore a matter of appreciating its fundamental significance and of envisioning the variety of ways it can be manifest in human life.

How Rich a Conception of Educational Aims? Two Answers at Odds

I begin with a take on how the question of the specificity of educational aims can confound debate. Philosophers such as John White believe educational aims should be so specified as to direct the actual practice of educators in formal schooling. White calls for the demarcation of rational, substantial curriculum objectives to the extent that the broader aims carry "statutory force" (2007: 1, 46). His view may therefore be dubbed a radical practicalism.[1] In his contribution to the Philosophy of Education Society of Great Britain's *IMPACT* series, entitled "What Schools Are for and Why," White laments the British national curriculum's lack of coercive power, arguing that the curriculum has anyway outgrown its historical roots (Chapters 1–4). He supports the direct practical impact of official aims, recommending a "sound rationale" (9) for the curriculum[2] and a "reasoned explanation" of how its aims and values should "fit together in a coherent way" (23), as a "unified vision" (1; cf. Chapters 5–7). On White's view, educational aims must be specific enough to regulate practice and hold educators accountable. Otherwise, schools can afford to ignore the aims in favor of other actually "mandatory requirements" and so to remain, in effect, "all but aimless" (5). After all, if educational aims have no statutory force, what is the point of worrying about the broader nature and aims of education in the first place?

This is the angle of White's criticism of philosophers like Paul Standish. Standish argues in a chapter entitled "Education without Aims?" that it is a mistake to think the aims of education can be set out just so, because that would forfeit the ideality of the educational ideals in question. Take the aims of a liberal education in particular. Although the term is "elastic" and can apply to "a range of ideas in education" (Standish 2016: 113), it is reasonable to suppose this is due to a general understanding in the Western philosophical tradition—expressed most classically, perhaps, in Plato's allegory of the cave—that education involves developing authentically free individuals, the word "liberal" deriving from the

Latin *liber* (free).³ It would then be no accident that the idea goes back to "Socratic self-criticism and critical thought about one's own traditions. As Socrates argued, democracy needs citizens who can think for themselves rather than deferring to authority, and who can reason together about their choices" (Nussbaum 2009: 10). In contemporary discourse about liberal education, emphasis is often placed on autonomy or rational freedom as a seminal aim, where education is supposed to culminate in the capacity to make autonomous, rational choices over a range of alternative visions of the good life.⁴ Standish, however, warns against succumbing to the "formalism" that often pervades discussions of this sort; he would have us beware of the discourse's "tacit assumptions," "epistemological presuppositions," and "self-perpetuating language" of "clarity and enlightenment," "precision," and "evidence" (1999: 39–40). He argues that contemporary discussion on liberal aims exhibits a kind of "self-referentiality" (40), even a "monologism" (48), that deadens "sensitivity to context, to variety and to individual potential" (43), by attempting systematically to shape education in its own image. In other words, we should be careful not to over-intellectualize notions like "rational" and "freedom": we risk romanticizing the lifestyle familiar to academics, those who have deigned to engage in this discussion in the first place; but a fisherman, too, is rational and free, and can lay equal claim to be enjoying the good life, even if he is simply taking up the family trade.⁵

As against the common assumptions of modernity, in the ancient Greek conception of a liberal education the "idea of the good is approached not by explicit demarcation but through a kind of lyrical intimation" (Standish 1999: 44). Standish advocates a return to this. He emphasizes the indirect and self-effacing "erotic perfectionist longing" that pervades Plato's dialogues (43–6), such that "the kind of reality which God and the good are conceived to have is an open question" (48).⁶ The general aim, if it can be so called, of a liberal education then becomes an ideal whose ideality, or ineffability, is only transgressed by systematic treatment. Standish suggests a renewed attention to "the purposiveness of human activity" and to the particular human relationships that unite teacher and learner (42). That would be to promote the "substantive nature of the contemplation required by Plato's theory of the Forms" (37) and to resist the "top-down setting of aims in favour of a bottom-up approach arising from the learner's activities themselves" (43). Standish concludes that

> the attempt to name the good is an attempt to identify something mysterious and marvelous. This has proved unsayable, other than in opaque, negative and oblique ways. ... This is not merely a matter of style.
>
> (47)

> A literarily crafted philosophy of education would open the possibility of a way of thinking which would unsteady the discourse of liberal education. It would do this not to jettison liberal education but to resist the limitations to which its monologism makes it subject. In doing so it would keep liberal education open to that ancient sense of the good which modern formalistic or naturalistic tendencies have subdued or obscured. Sceptical of the direct representation of the good it would locate itself in a recollection of what has been said before, in a response to texts going beyond anything which could be made fully present. Its withholding and humility, sometimes its renunciation of the claim to know, would themselves be characteristics of that intimation of the good which defies clear statement in a set of aims. This is the kind of thing in which teacher and learner might well be enthralled.
>
> (48)

Responding directly to Standish's chapter, White argues that while he can appreciate a healthy distrust of the "over-prescriptive specification of objectives," he still believes Standish's "positive alternative is too under-described either to act as a guide for educators or to enable us to see its compatibility or otherwise with liberalism's autonomy aims" (White 1999: 187). White is willing to entertain the notion of liberal education as a kind of "spiritual ascent towards the Good," but complains that, "if we are to entertain it, it must be given more shape. For how otherwise could such an aim be safely brought into the educational world?" (187). Standish's refusal to fix the course of the "liberal" in liberal education is unacceptable for White because it allows too much for the possibility of misguided educational practices—for "Platonic mystics, Christian theologists, deep ecologists and adherents of all kinds of exotic cosmologies to move into no man's land" (187–8). This is all he has to say here about Standish's view, but a few years later he writes, "Philosophy of education, or so I have always thought, is intended to have some bearing on education as it is actually conducted. But how, given Standish's highly indeterminate account of education, could the gear wheels ever intermesh?" (White 2003: 155).

Note the rhetorical force of White's criticism. How, he asks, could an aim so shapeless as the ineffable good be safely introduced to educational practice? How could a fundamentally indeterminate account of education do any real work? A terse rebuttal, perhaps, but need more be said? It is basic for White that educational aims be properly explicit. The realities of practice demand this. "The most important question to ask about school education is 'What is it for?'" (White 2007: 5). That is, at least implicitly, a question about the actual achievements of education. For White, aims must be explicit enough, secure enough to regulate the practices of educators and hold them accountable. How otherwise could we be sure that education is going to happen in the way that it should?

Standish, however, anticipates this response: "But must there be aims?" he asks in return. "The assumption that there must be accords with the principles of rational planning which in many respects characterize the modern world. The assumption that there must be invests in advance in that discursive form" (1999: 40). The automatic rhetorical power behind the rational aims discourse is exactly what Standish finds suspicious. The discourse supports the systematization of educational practice and its "language of objectives" (49) insofar as it only recognizes aims that are explicitly demarcated and have a statutory character. Of course it offers intellectual reassurance, and Standish acknowledges that his literary vision of education can appear useless, weak, indeterminate in the face of modern demand for control, assurance, accountability; but the contemporary aims discourse is only able to offer the "security of control" we expect today because it already concerns itself almost exclusively with the "accountability, quality assurance, objectives, performativity" (49) that are the trademarks of our time. In a world where efficiency is of the highest value, discussion about educational aims can allow itself to be presumptuous, self-referential, and self-perpetuating—to build on and at the same time reinforce demand for the systematization of educational practice. "When education is undertaken on a large, systematic scale ... skepticism about the giving of aims may seem like a kind of political irresponsibility. Surely there must be aims. And should these not be explicit?" (40–1). The rhetorical power of that response is exactly what Standish is challenging.

Put that way, it is far from clear whether White's criticism of Standish is appropriately incisive.[7] For Standish, the formalizing language of aims and objectives restricts thinking about educational ideals from the outset. The call to aims in education seems a mere product of history, the default emphasis on rational autonomy a stifling localism of Western modernity. Its self-referentiality should be questioned, "not to overthrow and replace but to complicate and destabilize, to test the limits of" (1999: 48). Like the ineffable good, we must emphasize the sheer ideality of educational ideals at the expense of the language of systems of control, and that means emphasizing the substantial, contextual, and spiritually rich nature of education. This requires cultural and intellectual humility and a willingness to admit possibilities that seem foreign to us.

On the other hand and for all that, White is anything but embarrassed about the localism, historical or otherwise, of his views. He insists unapologetically that the unavoidable complexities of contemporary Western society and the realities of large-scale educational practice demand careful reflection on what it means to be educated, what it means to be able to choose and to have a good and fulfilling life. Like it or not, education occurs "within a framework of democratic citizenship in which each person is equally valued and each person is free to make their own decisions about how they are to lead their lives" (White 2007: 25). For White, this entails an immutable requirement for a clear and comprehensive picture of how young people should be educated, of what education can actually achieve. Young people living in a democratic community are "citizens in the making," and their education should reflect this; it should reflect, for example, "such basic democratic values as political equality, self-determination, freedom of thought and action" (27). However parochial or self-referential, such is the reality that educators face today. For White, an account of education that fails to engage this reality by trying to focus on vague universals and indeterminate ideals remains, in practice at least, all but aimless.

The Impasse Concerning Educational Ideals

Debate along these lines can appear confounded, and perhaps hopelessly so. Philosophers who are sympathetic to White's approach will want to take as basic something like the following: (a) there must be a clear and coherent statutory relationship governing educational aims, curriculum objectives, and teaching practice; (b) the realities of living in Western society today demand a comprehensive discourse on rational aims with this relationship in view; and (c) the nature of that discourse means it is bound to say something affirmative and specific about liberal education as the development and actual achievement of autonomy, or rational freedom, in a liberal democratic society. Philosophers who are sympathetic to Standish's approach will want to emphasize something like the following: (a) the abstract ideality of educational ideals; (b) a connection between the ideal, the personal contextual, and the creative in education; and (c) the ancient conception of liberal education as an erotic progression toward and perfectionist longing for the ineffable good. Those who agree with White will see Standish's view as too vague or indeterminate to have any real bearing on educational practice; and, while recognizing the significance of the ideality of educational aims, they will locate it in the varieties of fulfilling lives that are available as options to an educated and therefore autonomous liberal democratic citizen; they will also see the self-referentiality of the discourse on rational aims as an unavoidable and perhaps salutary aspect of modern life in the liberal West.

Those who agree with Standish will see White's view as transfixed by, or fixated on, the modern formalist assumption that everything meaningful, including educational aims, must be made explicit; and, while recognizing the significance of practice to educational ideals, they will locate what is important about it in the contextual realities and human relationships that belong to teacher and learner, hence in the authentic educational enthrallment with the ineffable good; they will also see the self-referentiality of the rational aims discourse and related discussions about rational freedom as arrogant and suppressive of creative thinking about the possibilities of education, and of being human, elsewhere and in the future.

My summary of the exchange between Standish and White concerning the formalization of educational ideals may appear tokenistic; but I believe it is reflective of the widespread assumption that an answer to the question of educational aims is supposed to lie somewhere between, say, a rampant spiritualism and a regime of Orwellian uniformity. I do not advocate some final resolution to this dispute. The question about the substantiality of educational aims and their practical significance is, I think, importantly perennial. That is reflected in the underlying tension between the two principal insights at issue, namely, the ideality of educational ideals and the reality of education's achievements and demands. A perennial impasse is intolerable, however; but it might be unavoidable if the discussion were to retain its present one-dimensionality. I believe it is possible to relieve some of the tension here by recognizing a basic duality in the very idea of an educational aim, in a way that will preserve something of the main insights from both sides of the debate. To this I now turn.

Rational Freedom as a Transcendental Educational Ideal

The duality as I see it is like this. The nature of educational ideals is that they are at once transcendental and impossible. That is to say, real, actual achievements of education can be called basic insofar as they are fundamentally constitutive of what it is to live a human life, but what those achievements might really amount to, or how they might manifest themselves, remains essentially an open question. Put another way, the ideality of educational ideals is informed by their transcendental origins.

To understand what I mean here by "transcendental," consider the case of rational freedom.[8] Suppose we say with David Bakhurst that it is the capacity, distinctive of humans and basic to our being, "to make up our minds what to think and do in light of what we know to be true and good" (2011: 124; compare Bakhurst 2012: 174, 187). We might then insist that it is a precondition of our understanding of any human life—not that rational freedom stands alone as a fundamental human power, but that no life is recognizably human without its involvement.[9] If we were to say further that a basic achievement of education is an individual's coming to exercise her natural powers of rational freedom, that would be to make a transcendental claim about rational freedom as an educational ideal.

At the very least, then, a liberal education of any kind is supposed to involve cultivating this basic capacity. Now if it is true that the guiding insight of the rational aims discourse is the reality of education's achievements and demands, what do proponents of rational freedom think education really achieves in achieving it? Of concern is whether, or the way in which, rational freedom is seen by its proponents strictly as a fundamental achievement of education—or whether the underlying concern is actually to promote it as a substantial, codifiable aim. When, as in much contemporary discourse on liberal education, philosophers point to rational freedom as the preeminent aim of education, they can appear vulnerable to Standish's objection that it is a predominantly Western intellectualist preoccupation that by no means need apply universally. Perhaps some or many such philosophers, including John White, are indeed so vulnerable insofar as they promote rationality—for example in the form of critical thinking—as a discrete skill whose attainment facilitates our opting over alternatives of the good life.[10] If, however, rational freedom were understood more basically as a transcendental achievement of education everywhere, where being reasonable and meaningful at all originates as a bare possibility, and where that possibility already manifests in everything that is recognizably human, then it is not clear that the objection holds in the way it is meant to. This in turn may point to a way of understanding rational freedom as a real achievement of education, without recourse to the objectionable view that its legitimacy as an aim depends either on its statutory impact or the extent to which it can be described in a systematic manner.

Consider as an example Israel Scheffler's reply to an interview question from Harvey Siegel.

Siegel: There are some theorists who would argue against the very idea of rationality, as conceived in the Western philosophical tradition, that it has unhappy political consequences or presuppositions; in particular, that it in effect imposes a Western, "masculinist" conception of rationality onto people who have different cultural values and cultural and gender identities and so on. Do you have any sort of general reaction to that?

Scheffler: Yes. That kind of argument seems to me ridiculous, to put it straight. … In the first place, the justification of rationality is not that it promises "happy" political consequences, but that it empowers understanding, effectiveness in action and the pursuit of truth.

(Siegel 2005: 649–50)

Scheffler's curt response to this challenge is reminiscent of White's response to Standish, and can seem equally arrogant. It is, after all, self-referential in just that sense against which Standish urges caution. Scheffler, however, means to be understood as advocating the fundamental significance of rationality as such, not only as a Western liberal democratic educational aim—and hence one that is either appropriately or else objectionably local—but as "peculiar in that it is applicable in all realms in which one can sensibly ask for the reason, or reasons, why, including the practical, the moral, the ethical, the aesthetic and the domain of skills" (649). This means rationality in its most basic sense should be understood as germane to all realms of human experience, activity, and understanding, not as a particular political or cultural standard held up to signify, measure, or advocate educational excellence, as though "rationality is a Western trait imposed on the reluctant East, for example"—a supposition Scheffler calls "ludicrous" (650). That is why he can say, evidently without regret, "[p]olitical, cultural, and gender critiques are wildly beside the point" (650) and "utterly irrelevant to rationality" (651). Scheffler regards such critiques as objections "not to rationality as such but rather to the way it is presumed to have been conceived," in this case as a Western intellectuallist, masculinist preoccupation (651). Rationality, understood in more elementary terms, is basic to human being and therefore a fundamental achievement of education everywhere. Thinking is the manner of human being.[11] It is transcendental in that it is already involved, presupposed, in everything human.

Despite Scheffler's claims, however, it is clear that rationality has in fact been conceived far beyond this elementary sense. It is an empirical truth that rationality has been conceived substantially according to gendered, sexual, ethnic, colonial, psychological, religious, political, cultural, economic, and historical motives and presuppositions, with all their attendant logical, metaphysical, and otherwise self-referential philosophical superstructures. Centuries of literature and history attest to this—to say nothing of cognate attitudes popular even today.[12] It is not totally plain, moreover, that Scheffler does restrict himself only to the transcendental point about rational freedom.[13] "A rational man," he declares in *Reason and Teaching*,

> is one who is consistent in thought and in action, abiding by impartial and generalizable principles freely chosen as binding upon himself. Rationality is an essential aspect of human dignity and the rational goal of humanity is to construct a society in which such dignity shall flower, a society so ordered as to adjudicate rationally the affairs of free rational agents, an international and democratic republic.
>
> (1973: 76)

This statement goes beyond the bare assertion that rational freedom is a transcendental educational aim. Scheffler describes rationality as basic to human dignity, but proceeds to draw a more robust picture of the "rational man" as someone imperturbably logical, resolute, and self-transparent. Nobody is really like that, but however we may wish to criticize the substance of Scheffler's view, the fact is any unqualified promotion of rational freedom such as his is bound to be understood as firmly in line with the formalist assumptions of which Standish is critical. It is one thing to make the basic point about rationality as such, but it is another to deploy the transcendental argument in support of the educational primacy of rational freedom or autonomy, if that is going to be understood even implicitly as a reifiable, codifiable goal of education from a traditional Western "intellectualist" perspective. That is why Standish's and other ostensibly "wild," "ridiculous," and "ludicrous"[14] critiques of the rational aims discourse and of the notion of rational freedom in particular as an educational aim remain appropriate to the discussion.

Consider another example. Paul Hirst, in a memorable chapter entitled "Education, Knowledge and Practices," renounces his earlier view that rational freedom is the highest goal of education and the ideal to which all human activity should aspire. "The justification for that notion of the good life," he recalls, lay

> in certain forms of transcendental argument, which held that there can be no more ultimately justifiable pursuits than the intrinsically worthwhile pursuit of reason in all its forms, and, second, in the ordering of all other human concerns in terms made possible by the achievements of reason into a coherent and consistent whole.
>
> (1993: 185)

Note the continuities here between Hirst's former view and the view espoused by Scheffler. Both views draw their strength from the transcendental argument about rational freedom, but they lay claim to the argument in order to promote a more substantive picture of what rational freedom should amount to. Hirst no longer considers the notion of the good life described here to be justified, however, because he no longer thinks the pursuit of rationality *per se* presides transcendentally over all other "justifiable pursuits." He has given up the traditional notion of autonomy, understood as something that "marks out operationally, and perhaps even metaphysically," a subject that is "self-determining and self-directing, able to achieve rational understanding, make rational choices and take rational actions" in an "objective, disinterested" way (125). He now advocates placing rational autonomy squarely within the practical sphere, where the satisfaction of shared social, psychological, physical, and otherwise natural needs, desires, and interests is of the most basic importance. "A good life is in these terms a rational life," he writes, "but one ordered by the demands of practical reason, not those of theoretical reason as the advocates of rational autonomy have understood those. Nor is it a life characterized by autonomy as they have understood that" (130).

The fact that Hirst has abandoned that particularly modern and liberal notion of "autonomy" in favor of "practical reason" is more evidence suggesting that, contrary to Scheffler's claims, rational freedom has scarcely been seen by its proponents only as a transcendental achievement of education. It seems instead that the self-referentiality of the rational aims discourse has led modern liberal educational theorists to deploy the transcendental argument in support of more substantive conceptions of rational freedom than the argument bears. Those conceptions have been partial to the generous theoretical assumptions of the discourse itself, as Standish points out, and as Hirst admits. Now that such conceptions are being challenged, however, and now that the transcendental claim is no longer seen as obviously supporting them, philosophers like Hirst feel forced to give up the more elementary conception of rational freedom for something apparently more defensible and at the same time substantial enough "to structure the content of education" (1999: 131). This remains firmly within the realm of the modern rational aims discourse insofar as it continues to advocate for a set of codified aims with which to regulate educational practice. More importantly, however, it says nothing unfavorable about the transcendental claim of rational freedom itself—only that it does not directly support the statutory objectives of that discussion.

Given its ambivalent and questionable relationship to the rational aims discourse, it is understandable that there is confusion about the status of rational freedom as an educational ideal. Even Standish agrees in *Beyond the Self* that "autonomy is obviously connected in a fundamental way with many aspects of our freedom and with the related notion of our individuality" and is therefore in some sense "a normal feature of the lives of mature human beings" (1992: 209). It is just that its modern conception "harbours a fallacy of a metaphysical kind" (210). The problem, I claim, is that promoters of rational freedom tend to impair its integrity as a transcendental achievement of education by associating it, directly or indirectly, with a more substantial notion already oriented by the goal of demarcating rational aims. In place of this, what is needed is a restored sense of how rational freedom can be a transcendental achievement of education, but without the added assumption that, in order to be considered legitimate, it must be described systematically or broken down into discrete curriculum objectives. What is needed is to be able to acknowledge rational freedom as a perfectly genuine educational ideal and a real accomplishment of education everywhere, but to refrain from seeing what is genuine about it as having to issue from its specificity or statutory consequence. Far from that, a transcendental conception of rational freedom should already speak to its ideality—to its remaining essentially an open question.

Ideality 1: "Rational Freedom" Is Radically Underdetermined

So far I have tried, first, to indicate how the question of the specificity or substantiality of educational aims, if taken one-dimensionally, can appear hopelessly confounded. I then introduced a duality perceptible in the very idea of an educational aim, by identifying the principal insights as somehow complementary. I suggested that the reality of an educational achievement like rational freedom could be chalked up to its basic, elementary, or transcendental involvement in human being. I also tried to show how proponents of rational freedom are tempted to promote a reified, codifiable conception by appealing to its transcendental nature. I then called for a restoration of the sense in which rational freedom can be understood as a fundamental achievement of education without recourse to specificity or statutory consequence.

Now I want to expound upon my most recent claim, the claim that the transcendental conception of a genuine educational ideal, such as rational freedom, informs its ideality such that the question what it amounts to remains essentially open. There are two main considerations that I have in mind. The first is the sense in which the ideal *per se* leaves open and underdetermined the substantial ways in which it can come about or be understood. Rational freedom is transcendental insofar as it is supposed to apply universally to human experience and understanding. It is a precondition of our recognizing a human life as such. The possible realities of human experience and understanding remain essentially open, however, and so do the possible manifestations of rational freedom; but this renders rational freedom profoundly ideal in a way that is already harmonious with Standish's conception of the ideality of the good in ancient liberal education—that is, as "an open question" (1999: 48).

Rational freedom's nature as an impossible aim thus seems to follow directly from its status as a transcendental achievement. It resists explicit or fixed demarcation insofar as, in actual experience, what may be reasonable or meaningful to think or do is always an interesting question. Any situation we find ourselves in presents us with an untold host of possibilities for thought, speech, and action; and we are highly adept at improvising and tailoring our responses in astonishingly subtle ways, for the sake of all kinds of motivations. The realm of art, perhaps especially of performance art, attests to this at nearly every turn by routinely producing very minute differences in tone and mood. Yet even in our ordinary daily lives there is no limit to the ways that remain available for us to act, react, and interact. Whether we actually do or not, we can always ask what is reasonable to think or do in the here and now.[15]

One might object here that the term "impossible" is a misleading description of rational freedom's ideal nature, and that what I really mean is "infinite," in the sense of Sebastian Rödl's discussion of health as an "infinite end" in *Self-Consciousness*.[16] This is a helpful comparison and worth exploring; but unless I am misunderstanding that discussion, I do not think that the infinity of infinite ends is equal to the radicalness of reason's ideality. In his book, Rödl describes practical reasoning as ultimately underpinned by infinite ends, which are not exhausted by their explaining what I do. This is in contrast to finite ends, which are so exhausted:

> A finite end is something I have not yet got. Wanting health is not like this. In full health, I want to be healthy. One feels like saying that health is an end *I have already achieved while being after it*.
>
> But one may also want to say that health is an end *I never achieve*. ... My want to repair a bicycle exhausts itself in explaining my actions; it is the cause of its own extinction. An end such as health, by contrast, does not expend itself in explaining what it explains.
>
> (2007: 36; original italics)

My description of the aim of rational freedom as exhibiting a duality does seem to fit neatly with Rödl's dual description of infinite ends insofar as I want to say of reason, as of health, that it "is an end I have already achieved while I am pursuing it, and that it is an end I never achieve as long as I am pursuing it" (36). It is true that reason does not expend itself in explaining human activity. Reason supports an infinity of manifestations and so it is an infinite end to exactly that extent. Rödl's explanation, moreover, of the apparently paradoxical nature of infinite ends is also valuable to our considering reason's ideality:

> Is wanting health a paradox, then? No; but it is not a finite end. It does not admit of the contrast that defines finite ends: of being on the way toward and having reached the end. A paradoxical description suggests itself when we attempt to conceive of health through this contrast and thus attempt to represent it as a finite end. An end to which the contrast of pursuing and having got does not apply is an *infinite end*.
>
> (36)

It would be absurd to think of health as a finite end, and it would be equally absurd to think that of reason, because there is no properly applying the contrast between pursuing and attaining that is definitive of finite ends. It is important to acknowledge this because the widespread impatience with philosophy in particular and the humanities in general is founded on the erroneous assumption that its ends are finite, as though philosophy should have long finished its centuries-old construction project, for example: but if philosophy is building a bridge, it is a bridge to God.[17] Anybody who has engaged with the philosophical tradition can see that there is no end to the possibility of seeing things anew, despite many attempts to end philosophy itself or to secure for it an absolute starting point. As Bakhurst puts it,

> Philosophy is an activity with ends that are internal and infinite. Some philosophers have believed that they could conclude philosophy, but this is a conceit. Philosophical insight and understanding are real, but they are always provisional, so there is no quieting the impulse to philosophical inquiry. Philosophy has no terminus—its object is one of infinite depth. ... This is the case, of course, not just for philosophy, but many activities, including education, which, when viewed in the ideal, also has no terminus.
>
> (2018: 97)

In light of these affinities with Rödl's conception of infinite ends, it is tempting to stop at the term "infinite" to describe rational freedom as an educational ideal. After all, it is true that the term "impossible" can mislead: it would be bizarre to claim that rational freedom is an impossible aim in the straightforward sense in which painting a round square is a logical impossibility.

There is, however, a unique tension in the concept of reason that should bring us to admit that the aim of rational freedom remains underdetermined in a yet more radical sense than an infinite end such as health. We can, with Rödl, say the following of health: "Now suppose I want health. I do not want it in the way a sick man does; I do not want to *become* healthy. Imagine me perfectly healthy: I may still want health. Perhaps I want not to be healthy but to *remain* healthy?" (2007: 35; original italics). We cannot say this of reason, though, because there is no telling what it is to be perfectly reasonable: we cannot conceive, achieve, and maintain perfect rationality in the way we might conceive, achieve, and maintain perfect health; and we really do seem to want to become reasonable in the way a sick man wants to become healthy, just as Socrates claimed no wisdom in seeking that.[18]

The love of wisdom for which philosophy is named is the longsuffering pursuit of something one does not possess, not the cherishing of a treasure one has acquired and wishes to keep safe. This is the more radical sense in which there is no end to becoming educated. Even though the possible manifestations of health and the ways of pursuing it are infinite, we know what it is to be healthy: it is not internal to the concept of health that our understanding of it be provisional. That characteristic does seem internal to the concept of reason, however, insofar as what purports to be reasonable is always open to critical reflection, but where the very faculty of reflection is at once what is reflected and what is doing the reflecting. A circumstance of this kind opens the way to philosophical experiences that, as I argue in Chapter 5, can be deeply transformative. Such is the nature of self-consciousness, and such is reason's centrality to it. Reason, if it is a transcendental aim of education and of philosophy, is an impossible end—not just in the sense that it is never exhausted by the completion of tasks in its pursuit, but in the sense that its very nature always invites critical reflection.

Note that this is no relativism about reason, but an acknowledgment of reason's ongoing responsibility to itself. If in education we inherit a "store of historically accumulated wisdom about what is a reason for what," then, as John McDowell writes, our "tradition is subject to reflective modification by each generation that inherits it. Indeed, a standing obligation to engage in critical reflection is itself part of the inheritance" (1994: 126). If education in a basic sense achieves the pursuit of the reasonable and the meaningful, like the pursuit of the good, then it is a standing truth that what is reasonable and meaningful and good is open to question. The achievement of rational freedom through education not only introduces the bare possibility of being reasonable or meaningful in the here and now: it initiates as a standing issue the contemplation and reflective criticism of those very ideals. This means an educational ideal such as rational freedom, understood transcendentally, is genuinely achievable, but the aim is also impossible insofar as its substantive practical and conceptual manifestations remain essentially, radically open.

Ideality 2: "Rational Freedom" Is Not a Standalone Aim

This brings us to a second consideration about the ideality of rational freedom: it is by no means the sole elementary achievement of education. Its cultivation is not the only thing that transpires. Other ideals exist that are also basic to human being, and rational freedom is itself inextricably related to a whole family of concepts that need to be in play in order for us to appreciate a life as human.[19] Rational freedom becomes fantasy when abstracted away from the real possibilities of human experience and understanding; and its individual maximization at the cost of those other fundamental achievements is a worthless goal.[20] I do not believe rationality itself can even be understood apart from them: it is "inevitably embedded in a web of meanings" (Standish 1992: 194) whose threads they themselves are. That is a transcendental claim about the mutual presupposition of a family of concepts involved in our understanding a human life as such. They include, in no particular order, rational freedom, meaning and value, virtue and morality, materiality and historicity, practical reasoning, the practical and social nature of language, spirituality and existentiality, emotion and mood, art and creativity, selfhood and self-knowledge, the other, and the community—and, we should add, the understanding and pursuit of the good, the beautiful, and the true. When we talk about people, both particularly and in general, these concepts combine and come apart and rearrange themselves in a multitude of unique and interesting ways. To inquire into the transcendental nature of rational freedom is to inquire into a whole complex of fundamental educational achievements, and that means seeing those achievements together in their ideality, the way in which their individual maximization at the cost of the other ideals is simply unavailable. This makes rational freedom impossible as a standalone aim.

One might insist that there is an important sense in which rational freedom is the preeminent educational ideal, on account of the extent to which reason defines the human life-form. I am inclined to agree that reason is the all-embracing end of education. If that is so, however, it can only be in the transcendental sense—as the unifying principle of a family of mutually presupposed concepts such as those described above. Emotion, morality, practical reasoning, artistic creativity, and so forth would then fall under this broad view of rationality. Any narrow conception of rational freedom, for example under the guise of critical thinking, must then be conceived as just one aim among others and therefore impossible to maximize. If rational freedom is the preeminent educational ideal, it cannot glorify critical thinking above other forms of rational behavior, because as a unifying principle it must embrace within it the entire manner of human being—thinking—in all its varieties. To conclude otherwise would be to lose sight of the difference between the transcendental conception of rationality and that narrower notion. It would be to repeat the mistake of deploying the transcendental argument in favor of a specific conception of rationality.

The above is just a sketch of what might be called the structural duality of educational ideals. In a phrase, the duality consists in their status as the transcendental origins of impossible aims. That is, they are at once actual and ideal. My hope is that recognizing this duality will ease some of the tensions that exist between polarized and polarizing views about the specificity, substantiality, or richness of educational aims. The effect of this should be a reconciliation of the two principal insights at issue, namely, the reality of education's achievements and demands, and the ideality of educational ideals. Any understanding of this duality must recognize the following: (a) the way in which ideals such as rational freedom stand as genuine, fundamental achievements of education; and at the same time (b) the way in which these achievements, understood as applying universally to human life, are also profoundly ideal in the sense that (i) they are elementary concepts the manifestations of which remain essentially open to question and (ii) they are each inextricably related to a whole family of ideals that stand together as fundamental and yet underdetermined achievements of education, and therefore defy individual maximization at the cost of the others.

The conceptual unity of education itself seems to deteriorate if we try to pull its basic ideals apart and focus too much on one or another in an attempt to maximize those ideals individually. The ideals are meaningful only in relation to one another and in their unity in the individual—the thinking being. More than that, their unified ideality already informs the impossibility of their maximization. This should not seem very astonishing: it speaks to the endless varieties and possibilities of living a meaningful and fulfilling human life that our freedom makes available to us. Our understanding of the transcendental significance of educational ideals such as rational freedom is at least as open ended as their practical manifestations.

Conclusion: The Duality Applied to Other Work in Educational Philosophy

If it is appropriate and helpful to view educational ideals as bearing out this dual structure, it is important that we understand the writings of philosophers such as David Bakhurst under its framework. Otherwise we stand the chance of falling back into the one-dimensional, polarizing debate with which I began this discussion. When Bakhurst, at the conclusion of *The Formation of Reason*, describes himself as having "defended the view that the end of education is autonomy" (Bakhurst 2011: 158), he can easily be read as obstinately promoting the statutory objectives of the modern rational aims discourse—or as placing autonomy over rationality, for example, in educational consequence. For some this may make his position seem a little uncomfortable, but we need not feel that way.

Bakhurst goes so far as to acknowledge that there are "continuities" between his view and "the idea of liberal education expounded by the London School," including the idea of autonomy, quoting Standish, as "internally related to a rich conception of the development of mind through initiation into public modes of thought and engagement in worthwhile activities" (Bakhurst 2011: 142). Nevertheless, he is also keen to distance himself somewhat from the London School's views and especially from the views of some of its successors, including John White.[21] Bakhurst's claim that autonomy is the end of education is a claim about education's fundamental achievements, about rational freedom as a "fundamental power"—but he thinks it "cannot be treated formally and schematically" (124) as a reifiable or codifiable aim. The life that we are thrown into is unavoidably one characterized by rational freedom, but it is a standing issue just what that means and how it might possibly manifest in a human life. Through education

> we emerge as rational beings already possessed of views about the good, however partial, confused or incoherent they may be. Our task is to bring those views to consciousness and subject them to critical thought. ... To idealise this as the unencumbered choice of free individuals is to distort the situation in which we find ourselves.
>
> (143)

When Bakhurst writes, therefore, of an "autonomous subject of a life, self-conscious, responsible, creative," he means to conceive of that using a "socio-historical approach" and without recourse to "the myth of individuals as ready-formed and self-contained prior to society," or of "a domain over which reason's control is total" (2011: 151). In fact, on his view, what makes us individuals is precisely that the particular historical and cultural accumulation of wisdom about what is reasonable, meaningful, and good, from which and into which we emerge through education, is "for us a possible object of criticism" and of "reflective endorsement" (151). This is what he means when he tells us "problems of cultivating autonomy and the search for authenticity are sides of the same coin" (143). Seeing rational freedom as a transcendental achievement of education means seeing as a standing issue what that means at all and what it involves in the day-to-day of human living.

Although Bakhurst does not pay explicit attention to the duality I have been describing in this chapter, we can see his position is naturally sympathetic to it. This becomes clear from how and to what extent he wishes to respect John McDowell's "thin teleology" (Bakhurst 2011: 9) when invoking the term *Bildung*—German for what we might call "cultivation," "education," or "formation"—to describe the formation of mind. For McDowell, *Bildung* is the process through which emerges "an autonomous, critical rational agent 'at home in the world,'" but he "offers no account of *which* of the many ways in which a life can manifest rational autonomy are worthy of cultivation" (9; original italics). At the same time, McDowell's view of what *Bildung* actually achieves is "very strong": "It is the process of the coming into being of a self able to engage in practices of self-making" (9; cf. McDowell 1994: 125–6). The simultaneous "strength" and "thinness" of McDowell's view neatly translate to the structural duality I have been trying to recognize. We can take a "strong" view of ideals like rational freedom by recognizing them as transcendental achievements of education; but we can allow our view to be "thin" insofar as we recognize that those ideals remain an open question. In his account of the formation of reason Bakhurst aims to respect both that strength and that thinness, and near the end of his book he reaffirms his goal:

> So there is a sense in which the appeal to autonomy takes us everywhere and nowhere: it poses for us the question of what education should be and it demands a certain kind of answer—to equip us to live our lives determined by reason, where we can make up our minds what to think and do in light of what we know to be true and good. *How* to equip people for such lives is a question this book leaves open. Indeed, this could be said to be the great open question of educational theory.
>
> (2011: 124)

There is a sense in which the ideal of rational freedom poses a question that is at once inevitable and unanswerable. I said at the outset of this discussion that my intention would not be to answer directly the question of the specificity or substantiality of educational aims, but to alter its shape. The question seems importantly perennial, and now it is easier to see why. If rational freedom and every other transcendental achievement of education must be understood in their ideality, then a standing task remains for educational discourse to conceive appropriately rich conceptions of those ideals according to the changing conditions of history and the self-understanding of humankind. The perenniality of the question of education's substantial aims is indeed concerned with what, for us, constitutes a "worthwhile education" (Hirst 1993: 197)—but we should not conflate this with the longstanding question about what education "is" transcendentally. The idea that there is a family of transcendental ideals in education should not cause us to think it is worthless to debate what in practice an educated person should look like, for us today: in fact it demands such debate and at the same time reveals the question in its perenniality. To imagine that the aims of education can be fixed is senseless, but so is it to think that education achieves nothing real. It is a commonplace yet fundamental truth, in Bakhurst's concluding phrase, that "education makes us what we are" (162). What we are, though, is an open question.

Notes

1. Cf. Stefaan Cuypers's paper, "John White's Radically Practical Conception of Educational Philosophy," presented at the 2014 Philosophy of Education Society of Great Britain Oxford Conference. Cuypers calls White's view a "radically practical conception" (2014a: 2) not only because it envisions educational aims as having statutory consequence, but also because of its scope and magnitude, which puts educational philosophy on the level of global economic and social policy. The same phrase appears in Cuypers (2014b: 1).
2. This is not supposed to mean the curriculum as it presently stands. White explicitly leaves open whether the curriculum ought to remain as it is, especially as regards traditional classroom subjects.
3. Paul Axelrod, Paul Anisef, and Zeng Lin (2001) describe the concept of liberal education as "filled with paradox. It is at once the most enduring and changeable of academic traditions. It owes its origins to the philosophers and teaching practices of Ancient Greece and, arguably, continues to embrace certain core values from that era" (50). In the opening paragraphs of *Education's Epistemology*

(2019: 3–5), Harvey Siegel describes reason as enjoying a "virtually unanimous endorsement of historically important philosophers of education" (4), and proceeds to directly link reason with autonomy, or a person's ability to "judg[e] for herself the justifiedness of candidate beliefs and the legitimacy of candidate values" (5). C.f. Løvlie and Standish (2002: 324–5): "A first move in narrowing down the range of the expression is to consider what liberal education is to be contrasted with. Let us begin by accepting that a liberal education is unlike any education geared solely to extrinsic ends. It is at odds, it can also be agreed, with any conception of education that is not centrally concerned with the good of the learner, the notion of the good here being tied especially to conceptions of *freedom*. It is in virtue of this that it is liberal. … And freedom … in terms of the growth of mind, is not a natural condition but is a state to be moved towards through education. It is in this sense above all that a liberal education is free" (original italics). Compare also Bakhurst and Fairfield (2016: 1): "In such a context [i.e., in the "global 'knowledge economy'"] the once-hallowed ideals of 'liberal education' seem to have gone the way of the typewriter, the public telephone, and the seven-inch single—at best the object of affectionate nostalgia, at worst dismissed as obsolete. … Plato's cave allegory affords a classical articulation of the view repeatedly expressed in the history of philosophy that there is a higher purpose to education that must be conceived in ontological, not utilitarian, terms."

4   Harvey Siegel (1996; 2008; 2017, esp. chapters 1, 7, 11) and Christopher Winch (2002; 2006) are two prominent defenders of this view in the recent literature (cf. also Kotzee, Carter, and Siegel 2019; Gingell and Winch 2004, esp. chapters 1, 7). Of course, the London School, composed of R. S. Peters, Robert Dearden, and Paul Hirst, promoted rational autonomy as central to the concept of liberal education (cf. Dearden 1972).

5   Compare Paul Hirst's critique of abstract rational autonomy: "From this point of view the idea that a good life is one of rational autonomy is both inadequate and mistaken. The achievement of knowledge and understanding and the making of choices on abstracted rational grounds are in fact the satisfaction of certain very particular psychological needs and interests, those concerned to pursue abstracted, universal propositional truths, and principles. This pursuit is then being set above all others in a demand that all other forms of satisfaction, physical, psychological and social, be found only in practices that such propositional claims can formally justify" (1999: 128). I believe the likes of Jan Derry (2008; 2013) and David Bakhurst (2015) would—as I do—take issue with this particular characterization of rational autonomy and its relation to other aspects of the human lifeform—as though there were no other way to characterize it—but Hirst's critique of the traditionally abstracted view of rationality is not empty.

6   The term *eros* in philosophy has a much broader connotation than its manifestation in contemporary English. An "ongoing, asymptotic appreciation" might be a good way of understanding Standish's phrase here.

7   Nevertheless, the spirit of some of what White has to say about aims in education seems, on the face of it at least, in harmony with Standish's emphasis on the ideality of educational ideals and their discovery through particular human activities and relationships. In his *IMPACT* pamphlet, White writes of "a historically developing—and incomplete, needless to say—consensus on worthwhile pursuits" (2007: 42), a need for "grass roots rethinking of curricular patterns" (45) with more focus on "activities and relationships" (48), urging government to "positively encourage schools to diverge from traditional approaches" (47). Still, his insistence that "aims should be mandatory for schools" (48) and that they should have statutory force makes it questionable what an "over-prescriptive specification of objectives" (1999: 187) could really mean for him, even though he claims to agree with Standish that we ought to resist the latter.

8   I do equivocate here on "rational freedom," "autonomy," and "rationality"; but although not strictly identical, in their basic form these powers are a unity. Questions about this appear in the 2014 PESGB Oxford Conference Symposium on David Bakhurst's *The Formation of Reason* (cf. Siegel 2014). The following is from Bakhurst's unpublished reply during those proceedings: "On this view, we can think of reason and autonomy as powers. In fact they look like the *same* power: the power to determine what to think or do in light of reasons. But the powers can come apart, as it were. … So, I want to say that, when exercised properly, these powers coincide: they are a unity, but that their failings can pull them apart in contrasting ways" (2014: 2; compare Bakhurst 2011: Chapter 4). In *Education's Epistemology*, Siegel writes that the ideal of rationality "is thus a general ideal of a certain sort of person—the sort of person it is the task of education to help create. This aspect of the educational ideal of rationality aligns it with the complementary ideal of *autonomy*, since a rational person will also be an autonomous one" (2017: 5).

9   I use the term "involvement" here because there are those, like newborn infants and victims of severe brain injury, who do not exhibit the sort of rational freedom that we would generally expect even of a very young child; but to deny that these are human beings would be reckless. A human life is much more than its reductive scientific description as an organism in this or that mental and physical state at some particular time. To describe the life of a human being is to bring into view a whole world of meaningfulness and spirit—of stories, hopes, hardships, and loves past, present, and possible.

10 Cf., e.g., White (1990) and Siegel (1988), or more recently, Kotzee et al. (2019). As I indicate above, however, White seems to take the locality of liberal democratic educational aims as a reason for such codification with a view to achieving their

statutory force. Still, Standish's criticism of this way of thinking is profound. That is why I am attempting to restore a sense of rational freedom as a transcendental achievement of education without further recourse to more substantial, local norms. I do not mean to deny that the question of local educative norms is important.

11 I owe this phrase to David Bakhurst in conversation.
12 Cf., e.g., this recent study in *Collabra: Psychology*: "We tested the hypothesis that sematic [sic] associations, whether assessed explicitly or implicitly, link the concepts of *male* to *reason* and *female* to *emotion*. Our results provide evidence of robust semantic associations between both these pairs of concepts, thereby putting empirical teeth to a straightforward interpretation of a longstanding claim in feminist philosophy" (Pavco-Giaccia et al. 2019: 11; original italics). An obvious example of that "longstanding claim" of alterity is found in the opening paragraphs of Simone de Beauvoir's *The Second Sex* (1989): "A man is in the right in being a man; it is the woman who is in the wrong" (xxi); or more broadly, "Otherness is a fundamental category of human thought. Thus it is that no group ever sets itself up as the One without at once setting up the Other over against itself" (xxiii).
13 In the same interview, for example, he speaks of "the high value placed upon rationality" in a way that suggests an equation with being "intellectually serious" (Siegel 2005: 651) and with promoting "excellence in science, mathematics and technology and … the expansion of political power and trade" (650).
14 Note that these words are Scheffler's, cited in the paragraph above.
15 Compare Bakhurst: "So rational life is marked by the constant relevance of the question, 'How to act?' The inescapability of the Socratic question, 'How should we live?', is a mark of the human condition" (2018: 93–4).
16 I am grateful to David Bakhurst for suggesting this avenue of discussion.
17 Cf. the epigraph to Gadamer's (2004b) *Truth and Method*.
18 Compare Stanley Cavell (1979: 44): "In Wittgenstein's work, as in skepticism, the disappointment with human knowledge seems to take over the whole subject, … I might say that publicness is his goal. It would be like having sanity as one's goal. Then what state would one take oneself to be in?"
19 "The individual … can only be rational through his participation in the larger society, which is external to the self. … The abstracted notion of the self loses sight of this point" (Standish 1992: 189).
20 Cf. esp. Chapter 5, §5 of *Beyond the Self*. "The ideal of autonomy is a formal notion which is of limited value unless coupled with substantive notions about particular practices. … Presenting the ideal apart from these substantive matters encourages a valuing of choice for its own sake which is spurious" (1992: 194).
21 Bakhurst describes those views specifically as equating autonomy "with the ability to *choose*, specifically to choose how to live in a way that best satisfies preferences

that one has formed without coercion. On this view, education is charged with equipping individuals with the resources to form considered preferences and make unpressured choices about how best to satisfy them. ... On my account, the fundamental notion of autonomy ... [as the] the power to determine one's thought and actions by reasons is not primarily a power of choice. ... We are thrown into life and must find our way" (2011: 142).

5

Education and Transcendence: At Home in *Unheimlich* Language

I have said much about the philosophical nature of education, but not enough about the educative nature of philosophy, even though it has been a refrain throughout. I want to resolve this in the present chapter, where I argue that philosophy returns us to the original educative achievement by transforming our understanding of that which has long been familiar to us. I also bring together the main ideas of the foregoing chapters by offering a phenomenological model for the universality of language in relation to the self-conscious individual—the thinking being. In so doing, I take up Heidegger's suggestion that "language speaks solely and solitarily with itself" (2008c: 397–8). All this will serve as preparation for the brief concluding chapter, in which I suggest further that education wakes Being itself to its own thinking.

A theme of this book has been to try to reflect the self-conscious experience of living in historical language—the way language can irrupt and erupt spontaneously and with astonishing creativity, gathering insights together into a synoptic vision whose origins and endings are many and none, seeming to point everywhere at the same time—the way the thinking of mind, over any expanse of history and text, always returns to itself renewed because language speaks nourishingly. That hermeneutical revolution, which I am suggesting is education's original and unending achievement, and can be understood philosophically as transcendence, is *unheimlich* through and through. The experience of living in language is, I want to say, a continuous waking to thinking Being: it is an always coming to terms with reality in a way that is at once deeply familiar and not at all.

Themes and Theses and What Philosophy Can Mean for the Everyday

I began in Chapter 1 by pointing to a deeper connection between philosophy and education than is generally acknowledged. I suggested that this connection, which is special among the disciplines, lies in the unlimitedness of their interests—their coming to terms with reality at large. Chapters 2 and 3 were attempts at filling this thesis out, first by articulating education broadly as effecting a metaphysical transformation, and then by emphasizing its essentially historical nature. I argued that fundamental to a proper understanding of education is language, the repository of historical mind and the medium of understanding. Being introduced to language, a child comes to stand in the midst of Being: she comes to be at home in the world by being held out into the nothing, that dimension of reality called metaphysics, where world and history stand out for her as such.

Appearing repeatedly throughout those chapters was the suggestion that, despite the twentieth-century collapse of foundational thinking, philosophy can still arrive at fundamental insights about things. Such insights, which transpire within the infinite reach of language, do not just involve the unearthing of new, socially operable metaphors. They are genuine insights into the true sense of concepts, particularly those, like education, that are central to our self-understanding; but we must understand "true sense" in terms of the dynamic historicity of language and therefore as essentially provisional and responsive to further questioning. In Chapter 4, I tried to make this special task of philosophical discourse more explicit by recognizing a duality in the very idea of an educational aim. On the one hand, there is the longstanding question about the transcendental achievements of education—how we understand what it means to be educated, in the broadest possible sense. On the other, there is the local, perennial question about what that means for us now—what education, formal or otherwise, could or should look like in our society today. Those questions are not wholly distinct, but ignoring their differences leads to an impasse in the contemporary debate concerning the substantiality of educational ideals such as rational freedom. One side insists on the actuality of education's achievements, while the other insists on their ideality, the way in which they cannot be maximized conceptually or practically. Each side emphasizes its own genuine insight at cost to the other, whereas both are right: education makes us what we are, but what we are is an open question.

A related theme has been that philosophy, a distinctively human activity, is not some parasitic theoretical approach to that which really matters, namely, the various practical aspects of human life. This is not to deny that the everyday experience of being human is a threshing floor for the purported discoveries of philosophy; but it is to deny that philosophy stands over against ordinary human living. Philosophy is thinking *per se*: it is thinking about things in general from the inside of things in general, arriving at insights that can transform, from the inside, our view of what is already there. This capacity for transformative thinking is what distinguishes our mode of life among other sorts of beings. Only because we are thinking beings does our way of being stand out at all, and only because our own being stands out to us, the thinkers, can we live practically in the more and less intelligent ways that we do.

This idea of thinking transformatively from the inside acquires character and structure if we think of being minded as standing in the midst of Being. Our capacity to think implies that our views about what it means to exist, or how we might live, generally and in the here and now, can undergo transformation. Education is the original event of transformative thinking: it transforms us into the metaphysical beings that we are, by introducing us to historical mind through the language of thought. Philosophy, the endless pursuit of self-understanding and the undying love of wisdom, is not an attempt to escape from history but to understand it for what it is. True, we are rational beings who transcend our environment by thinking, but our transcendence does not involve stepping outside of world history. It involves recognizing world and history as such through education, whose breadth is exactly as universal as the breadth of philosophy. Together education and philosophy constitute the self-fulfilling activity of mind and language—even, I suggest, of Being itself.

It is therefore available for educators everywhere to take the observations of philosophy, however self-indulgent they may appear, as drawing attention to something hidden within the everyday activities of education. The idea is not to talk down to the educator from some higher level of analysis, but to awaken her to the monumentality of her own practice, so she can imagine for herself how to think and act in its light. Of course this can all sound so intoxicating and romantic, like the platitudinous tautologies of a valedictorian's speech to a class of graduating teachers: "Go now and do likewise. Transform metaphysically the Being of thy pupils!" That objection is flippant, but it has a point. It is an instructive caricature of the nature of philosophy's insightfulness, and it is based on an idea familiar from Wittgenstein in his early thinking, which appears also in his later thought: that philosophy, no longer a foundationalist discourse, simply rings hollow if it continues to speak positively in broad, even tautological terms.

Transcendence and the Transformative Same-Saying of Tautology

What is instructive about this caricature? It is true, for one thing, that the thinking of humans—physical, living, animal beings who are also rational and can think about the whole of reality, whatever that may amount to—is thoroughly romantic: being metaphysical, transcending by thinking, is an adventure on the universal stage. We should not shy away from this but support it wholeheartedly. The fundamental insights of philosophy, moreover, really do approximate tautology insofar as they aspire to the "true sense" of concepts, much as etymology recognizes the way in which words operate on a familial level and, out of the great wellspring of historical mind and through myriad manifestations, continue to say something like the same thing. The word "tautology," in fact, comes from the Greek *tauto* (the same) and *logos* (saying). The true etymological sense of tautology is that it is the "same saying": it is perhaps something like "true sense" itself.

The difference for philosophy is this. The same-saying of tautology need not be understood as it typically is, as grammatical redundancy or duplicitous rhetoric. Above all, tautology need not be understood as Wittgenstein understood it in the *Tractatus*—as that which simply "cannot be put into words" (2007: §6.522) because it "follows from all propositions" and therefore "says nothing" (§5.142). On that early view, the tautological propositions of logic, ethics, aesthetics, and metaphysics are "transcendental" in the sense of being unutterably "mystical"—"They *make themselves manifest*"—so that all we can do to take what they say seriously is pass over the mystical whole of language in silence (§§6.13, 6.421, 6.53, 6.54, and 7; original italics). We can now say something importantly different. We can now say "tautology," which "says the same," indeed "says nothing" insofar as it "says everything": but it accomplishes all this explicitly, by holding us out into the nothing, that special dimension of reality called metaphysics, and giving us a renewed view of everything, of beings as a whole. That, though, is just the distinctive experience of rational, historical beings such as ourselves, who transcend by thinking—not in some occult way but by simply being in the world and knowing that we are. Saying the sayings of tautology is the metaphysical-historical privilege and burden of thinking beings.

To see the difference this makes, take the opening line of the *Tractatus*: "The world is all that is the case" (§1). This is an explicit orientation to all and everything true: but not only is the proposition supposed to be true everywhere; its truth is supposed to be implied, spoken everywhere by language. To register its truth, however, we do not need to stand in mystical silence at the limits of language and history in an attempt to view the world from the standpoint of eternity (§6.45) or "timelessness" (§6.4311). The event of our understanding the proposition happens in language as language unfolds historically: the proposition is written, read, and understood by beings whose ordinary activities and experiences are situated in language. It is therefore no surprise that we can understand the ostensibly nonsensical propositions of the *Tractatus*, being able to use them "as steps—to climb up beyond them," before attempting to "throw away the ladder" itself (§6.54). The "beyond" of tautological understanding, though, is nothing less than more language, more life. The lonely Cartesian meditator, like it or not, is still a human being in conversation with the reader, or from another standpoint the author, of those arguments.[1] The sayings of the *Meditations* just as well as the *Tractatus*—replete with explicitly philosophical propositions, both—remain: we do not need to throw them away; we keep them with us; they abide; they "exist."[2] Existing, they remain open to question.

The mistake of the *Tractatus* was to think that, in order to view the world "as a limited whole" (§6.45) and so to get the true sense of it, we can only "transcend" (§6.54), "in silence" (§7), the tautological same-saying of language. Language, though, itself transcends precisely by speaking: it takes care of itself through its explicit, not silent, historical unfolding of Being—"*the transcendens pure and simple*" (Heidegger 1927: 85; original italics and stylization). Transcending the world by understanding it as a "limited whole" does not happen silently "outside the world" (Wittgenstein 2007: §4.12) but exactly within it: language is the house of Being; it is Being that can be stood-in-the-midst-of. As Heidegger writes, "Being itself is essentially finite and reveals itself only in the transcendence of Dasein which is held out into the nothing" (1929: 108). The nothing is simply the clearing of language. In that space we live and think. Language itself is the "beyond" of metaphysics.

Understood as an event of historical transcendence, "tautological" philosophical insight need not be called empty platitude: it can be, and already is, genuinely educational and a real part of living, growing language. We learn by thinking, and thinking is transcending, creatively in language, the limits of our own thought by recognizing the true sense of things in a new way. The word "transcend" comes from the Latin *trans* (beyond) and *scandere* (to climb). Education, the historical leading out and into the midst of Being, is the way language transcends, climbing beyond itself. Education's activities, I have argued throughout, are basically philosophical insofar as it gives us an orientation to reality at large, allowing us to transcend our environment by climbing beyond ourselves to a view of things in general. The questions and insights of philosophy, which make this general orientation explicit, are not meant to carry us madly away from everyday human living, but to help locate us, broadly speaking, in the scheme of things. This is not the achievement of some timeless and unchanging clarity but the sort of clarity achieved when thinking is brought explicitly to bear on itself; and that is something that happens, on a scale of every measure, in everyday human living. The great splendor of philosophy, of thinking *per se*, is its capacity to return us to where we began, to our ordinary experience of being in the world—with renewed insight, a transformed view of what has been there the whole time—and with a refreshed ability to talk about things in new and profound ways.

Wittgenstein puts it thus (1958: §129), and Gadamer quotes him approvingly (1963: 176): "The aspects of things that are most important for us are hidden because of their simplicity and familiarity. (One is unable to notice something— because it is always before one's eyes.)" That is a good way of describing the insights of philosophy. As I noted in Chapter 1, however, even in his later thinking it is not clear that Wittgenstein believes the insights of philosophy do anything more positive than dissolve therapeutically its own misunderstandings of language. Even though he is now "talking about the spatial and temporal phenomenon of language, not about some non-spatial, non-temporal phantasm," he still seems to think philosophy cannot be anything more than "a battle against the bewitchment of our intelligence by means of language" (1958: §108). "Philosophy," he writes, "may in no way interfere with the actual use of language. In the end it can only describe it. / For it does not give it any foundation either. / It leaves everything as it is" (§124).

It is true that philosophy cannot give language a foundation, because there is no such thing: language takes care of itself. What is objectionable, however, is Wittgenstein's residual tendency to view philosophy as somehow standing over against language, its task—what Gadamer calls "the self-healing of self-inflicted wounds, similar to the way the *Tractatus* had already proclaimed its self-negation" (1963: 177)—appearing and disappearing only when the misunderstandings of traditional philosophizing aggravate and are assuaged. Beyond this, Gadamer suggests,

> Perhaps the field of language is not only the place of reduction for all philosophical ignorance, but rather itself an actual whole of interpretation that, from the days of Plato and Aristotle till today, requires not only to be accepted, but to be thought through to the end again and again.
>
> (177)

Contrary to Wittgenstein, Gadamer argues that the "whole field of language" is always available to be cultivated for the nourishment of thought and, therefore, of human life. In "thinking through" it as a whole philosophy does not float freely over unsoiled language but positively transforms it and locates us afresh in its midst.

Educative Tautology and the Whole of Interpretation

How can we know this? We can know it by recognizing that the speech of insight, however broad and apparently platitudinous, is educational insofar as it comes from and returns to language in its mundane everydayness. Education itself involves the making explicit of the often-implicit rules and shared principles of conduct and thought—tautologies—by which a community operates. Consider a personal example.

> My three-year-old son asks me, "Dad, where is Grand-maman?"
> "She's gone."
> "Where did she go?"
> "Atlas, Grand-maman died."
> "Grand-maman died? Why?"
> "Grand-maman got sick and it was too much for her, so she died."
> "But where did she go after she died?"
> "She didn't go anywhere. When you die, you are no more."
> "Did she disappear?" he persists.
> "Well, her body got cremated. They burnt her body into ash."
> Atlas, entering that familiar but uncertain territory he cannot help but explore, asks with his finest nonchalance, "Why did they burn her body into ash?"
> "Because she didn't want her body to rot in the grave."
> "Why didn't she want to be rotten in the grave?"
> The love of my life, Sarah, interjects with a stern look at both of us: "Atlas, we don't need talk about that all the time."
> After a moment, Atlas presses on: "So, Grand-maman is gone?"
> "Well, she still lives in our hearts," Sarah suggests.

"Why does she live in our hearts?"
"We remember her … " I begin.
Sarah completes the thought: " … And so she still lives in our hearts."
"Like Heaven is in our hearts?"
"Like Heaven is in our hearts."

If that is already too metaphysical, consider a more mundane case. Imagine two fishing guides having a conversation about the differences between muskellunge and northern pike—two powerful Ontario sportfish that share similar qualities but can be easily mistaken in the mayhem following a strike.

> "The muskie has shoulders," says one, matter-of-factly. "It's stronger and heavier than the northern. Both are lunge fish but the northern usually hits the bait hard and might even set the hook on itself, whereas sometimes a muskie will just take the bait and swim right at the boat. You might not even know it's on till you see it right there in the water, four feet long. Always set the hook if you feel anything but the bait on your line. Always."
> "Isn't it that a muskie takes the bait from behind, but a northern takes it from the front?"
> "No, that's bullshit. Don't believe everything you hear."
> "But it was you who told me that!"
> "Well, don't believe everything I say, either. I'm a fisherman by trade, you know!"

Perhaps this is too leisurely. After all, one might object that philosophical hankerings and banal tautologies arise only when the toils of surviving no longer require our attention and are forgotten. Consider, then, W. E. B. Du Bois's description of the "Sorrow Songs" (1994: Chapter XIV) of slavery, what he calls "the voice of exile" (158):

> They are the music of an unhappy people, of the children of disappointment; they tell of death and suffering and unvoiced longing toward a truer world, of misty wanderings and hidden ways. … The songs are indeed the siftings of centuries; the music is far more ancient than the words, and in it we can trace here and there signs of development. My grandfather's grandmother was seized by an evil Dutch trader two centuries ago; and coming to the valleys of the Hudson and Housatonic, black, little, and lithe, she shivered and shrank in the harsh north winds, looked longingly at the hills, and often crooned a heathen melody to the child between her knees.
>
> (157)

Those spiritual songs, Du Bois continues, "tell in words and music of trouble and exile, of strife and hiding; they grope toward some unseen power and sigh for rest in the End" (159). None of this is empty abstractionism.

In each of the above cases, "I already have to use language full-blown" (Wittgenstein 1958: §120) in repeating the tautological expressions of people. Human coping requires our taking a broader view of things, and the rational freedom language affords through education is exactly that ability to universalize, to articulate tautology. In doing so, however, we do not arrive at or harken to insight from some place other than what Wittgenstein calls the "rough ground" of language (§107).[3] Language's rough ground is just the ordinary activity of rational beings—of those who live in the world and know they do, and hence for whom philosophy itself, simply thinking about reality at large, is a natural, distinctive activity. The normal and everyday thinking, speaking, and acting of such beings alter the shape of language and hence the future of thinking in all sorts of ways, great and small. "With its saying, thinking lays inconspicuous furrows in language. They are still more inconspicuous than the furrows that the farmer, slow of step, draws through the field" (Heidegger 1947: 265).

Because we are thinking beings whose inheritance is language, we can harken to its speech by taking it up as "a whole of interpretation." It anticipates this "taking up" not only insofar as the creative geniuses of history have been consciously sowing unspoken brilliance in language itself. More than that, language always anticipates thinking insofar as a whole array of historical mind is already available in the words we speak and in those concepts whose meanings we want more profoundly to understand. Either way the priority of history means the insights of philosophy are never completely settled but always await understanding and criticism: they too are a part of, and cannot but partake in, the rough ground of language and are liable to transform in a positive way the "whole of interpretation" itself by saying something fundamental about it. That is why language always asks to be "thought through again and again"—word by word, furrow by furrow.

Philosophy's Same-Saying

Philosophy, therefore, does approach tautology wherever it attempts to say "the same" by saying what language everywhere says. If it is true that "language speaks solely and solitarily with itself" (Heidegger 2008c: 397–8), philosophy just tries to harken to its speech: and yet, "What do we hear there? We hear language speaking" (411). Contrary to Wittgenstein's enduring belief that whatever "expresses *itself* in language, *we* cannot express by means of language" (2007: §4.121; original italics), we can say with Heidegger that "[l]anguage speaks by saying; that is, by showing. Its saying wells up from the once spoken yet long since unspoken saying" (Heidegger 2008c: 411). In other words, philosophy tries to bring to expression that which is everywhere expressed in language and therefore remains unexpressed.[4] Of course this tautological same-saying is nothing complete, because it is a broad vision of the true sense of an incomplete whole; but that is why philosophy must attempt to orient us again and again to reality at large by standing explicitly in its midst and harkening to the speech of historical mind. There philosophy becomes unfinished language tending to itself explicitly, always reflecting on itself—"The ceaseless weaving of the uneven water" (Reznikoff 2005: 25). Precisely because "everything flows" (Wittgenstein 1975: §54) does the saying of this saying require us to dwell on it and understand it again and again.

In our doing so—in our harkening to the "unspoken saying" of language, in our understanding it by standing in its very midst—does Being itself, "the transcendens pure and simple" that is implicit everywhere in all thinking and speech, come into view. We experience being held out into the nothing, where beings as a whole stand out for us. This happens in the original leading out of education, the advent of metaphysics and hence of Being as such. Philosophy in turn is just "metaphysics' getting under way, in which philosophy comes to itself and to its explicit tasks" (Heidegger 1929: 110). It is an attempt to turn and return toward that original educative transformation, precisely by attempting, again and again, to come to terms with reality—with Being itself. I believe this to be the ultimate learning experience.[5]

> To bring to language ever and again this advent of Being that remains, and in its remaining waits for man, is the sole matter of thinking. For this reason essential thinkers always say the Same. But that does not mean the identical.
> (Heidegger 1947: 264)

Saying "the same" but not "the identical" is exactly the sense in which language returns to Being itself and unfolds it explicitly. Insights into the true sense of things continue to speak to us "again and again" because language unfolds by folding out into more language. "When philosophy attends to its essence it does not make forward strides at all. It remains where it is in order constantly to think the Same" (238). The sayings of language say the same saying not by insisting emptily on some platitude but by speaking anew to historical beings in a variety of historical environments. We can return at once to the rough ground of language and to the most rarified insights of history with new and profound, historically enlightened understanding.

Thinking "the same" then is just a return from the nothing to the nothing, into which, as metaphysical beings, we are already held out: "We cannot be transposed there at all, because insofar as we exist we are always there already" (Heidegger 1929: 110). Our returning to "where we already are" is in language. Contrary to Wittgenstein, when we do so return we do not have to be silent about some mystical realization that simply cannot be put into words. Language grows and transcends itself by speaking just where speaking wants to fail, not out of an unthinking dread of "silence" but out of recognition of its fertility. "It is out of the unfolding of this 'same' as différance that the sameness of difference and of repetition is presented in the eternal return" (Derrida 2004: 290). Returning to where we already are, we can talk, meaningfully in new and exciting ways, about what it means to be human, what it means to be at home in the world and to live in language. We return "with a second dangerous innocence" (Nietzsche 1974: 37)—because looking into the face of the universe has burned the nothing itself into our gaze,[6] so that Being comes into its own as the *ibidem* of all language and thinking.

At Home in *Unheimlich* Language

So far I have suggested that the tautological sayings of philosophy, however flamboyant, can have a transformative impact on the rough ground of language and everyday experience. Thinking *per se* is the original metaphysical achievement of education, to which philosophy attempts to return again and again. The whole history of language is where such thinking abides as an open question, and the effect of our harkening to it is a transformed view of what is already there. Philosophy is nothing less than a monumental learning experience happening fundamentally in time—a returning from and to understanding, historically in the midst of Being. Yet every monument is a sepulcher. The idea of returning transformatively to "the same" implies that understanding itself resides in the unfamiliar because it is always on its own threshold: "the same" is never "the identical." This brings us to the suggestion that being at home in the world, the monumental achievement of education, is *unheimlich* through and through.

I have repeatedly described education and philosophy as fundamentally related. Their orientation to the world in general means they face together the crisis of self-identity, of coming to terms with reality—of being a thinking being and hence of being at all. Its experience is at once not very and yet deeply familiar, and I think the German word *unheimlich* is appropriate to this duality that is internal to being at home in the world by understanding language.

Unheimlich literally means "un-homelike" and translates to "uncanny," or "uncomfortably strange." As Sigmund Freud observes, although "*unheimlich* is obviously the opposite of *heimlich*, *heimisch*, meaning 'familiar,' 'native,' 'belonging to the home,'" it is not mere "intellectual uncertainty" (1919: 418). It is more than simply not knowing one's way about.[7] Importantly familiar and yet equally not; an uncomfortable, intimate secret once concealed and now brought to light; it is perhaps something like the uncovering of pudenda, external human genitalia, loose skinfolds literally named "shameful."[8] *Heimlich*, Freud writes, is "a word the meaning of which develops in the direction of ambivalence, until it finally coincides with its opposite, *unheimlich*" (421). The *unheimlich* is something so familiar that it has long remained concealed; and when it is brought out into the open and made explicit it strikes us deeply as something strange, unnerving, even dangerous—a kind of blasphemy against the sacred unspoken.

Through education we are led out into universality as such: we are exposed to the universe exactly insofar as the universe is exposed to us. That experience is *unheimlich*, but so is the whole ensuing experience of living in language, of being at all and knowing that we are. It is not, however, only a psychological effect or a mood liable to visit us now and again, say when trying to think sincerely about education or flowers or God—or when reading Dostoevsky or watching a Stanley Kubrick film, or when contemplating Alex Grey's paintings or listening to Tool. What is revealed in that intentionally uncanny experience is, I claim, a reflection of the basic character of dwelling in language. Understanding language at all, transcending Being by standing in its very midst, is fundamentally *unheimlich*.

We live in a home that is un-homelike because its character is transformation rather than foundation. Language is the house of Being, but it carries its own foundation-walls. That is part of its essentially historical, tautological same-saying, which says nothing and everything at the same time and returns us afresh and nourished to where we already are—transformed in our self-understanding. Language is not only the location of homecoming for the understanding but also the location of understanding's homelessness. We are always learning how to think and how to say: to say what we think and to think what is said, so that "all thinking about language is already once again drawn back into language" (Gadamer 1976: 62).[9] We are not the masters of our own house: we are only ever on the threshold, and the threshold is all we know.[10] Our educational, philosophical homecoming to the world and to ourselves is without end, just as the homecoming of language, explicitly out and into the midst of Being, is an endless beginning-to-think and beginning-to-say. What is *unheimlich* about being a thinking being is precisely "this continual coming-to-language of our being-in-the-world" (Gadamer 1967a: 239). It is the ceaseless unfolding of the Being of those who live in skin and who do so metaphysically, by knowing they do.

Self-understanding—metaphysics—is thus at once a great privilege and a great burden. "Know thyself": to understand this saying is already to be on the threshold of realizing historical finitude and the looming impossibility of total self-transparence—even of realizing death. That is because self-understanding, and understanding in general, happens in-the-midst and always returns to itself incomplete: it is the ceaseless crisis of the finite beings that we are. Again, transcending by being held out into the nothing is nothing other than standing in the midst of historical language. Only from here can we contemplate among all else our own animal finitude over against universality as such, and here we must admit, each of us to ourselves, that—to the whole of historical mind and to reality at large—we are as nothing. That is disquieting, even dangerous, a standing at the edge of an abyss: "and where does man not stand at an abyss? Is seeing itself not—seeing abysses?" (Nietzsche 1988: 177)

Yet there always stands creative language, whose living wellspring of infinite possibilities constitutes the health and freedom of mind. In language there already awaits the great health and free growth of an unceasing "convalescence,"[11] a "healing"[12] of the understanding that is always on the verge of more healing: it is always on the threshold of more understanding and more language, more health. "To be sure," writes Gadamer,

> knowledge, conceived as absolute self-transparency, has something fantastic about it if it is supposed to restore complete at-homeness in being. But could not a restoration of at-homeness come about in the sense that the process of making-oneself-at-home in the world has never ceased to take place ... ? This freedom is certainly not gained in the sense of an absolute transparency, or a being-at-home that is no longer endangered. ... Is not language always the language of the homeland and the process of becoming-at-home in the world? And does this fact not mean that language knows no restrictions and never breaks down, because it holds infinite possibilities of utterance in readiness?
>
> (1967a: 238–9)

Waking to an unceasing "becoming-at-home in the world" through language, we are called to make ourselves at home in our own homelessness. This, we can say with Gadamer, would be to "restore at-homeness in Being." It would be to do so by way of a dangerous freedom: the infinite freedom of creative language.

Homelessness

That we might "restore at-homeness in Being" by acknowledging our basic homelessness suggests two divergent but related conditions of "homeless" being. Heidegger alludes to these in his "Letter on Humanism": there is the homelessness that is "the symptom of the oblivion of Being," particularly now in the age of technology (1947: 242), where philosophy is so often reduced to mere "technique" (221); and there is "the essential homelessness of man" (244). The first corresponds to a banal "nihilism," the ignorant condition that is just unthinking "indifference" to Being itself (253). Nihilism in general is the belief in nothing at all, a kind of radical suspicion that, if not properly overcome, winds up simply negating all values and truth; banal nihilism in particular is indifferent even to itself and hence also to the nothing, the ungrounded ground of our metaphysical existence and the source of our essential homelessness—the truest nihilism there is.

How, though, could there be a "true nihilism"? Are not truth and nihilism fundamentally opposed? "Nihilism stands at the door," declares Nietzsche: "whence comes this uncanniest of all guests?" (1967: §1). We can overcome the negativity of nihilism as Nietzsche did, by actually turning and facing it, and seeing in it our own creative potentiality. That would be to transform banal nihilism into true nihilism, the affirmation of the nothing as the location of our essential homelessness, in light of which the nothing becomes the positive space of possibility and creativity. In doing so we turn and face exactly that which "nihilates"—the "question of the nothing," which always "puts us, the questioners, in question" (Heidegger 1929: 109). When we acknowledge our being put into question by the nothing—by our ability to transcend the world and ourselves historically by thinking at all, by living in language and having an orientation to reality at large—we affirm the positive truth of nihilism, of our essential homelessness. "There is essentially no limit to the experience of being, which, since Nietzsche, we call nihilism" (Gadamer 1967a: 238). Hardly a thing to be ashamed of, acknowledging this *unheimlich* truth takes real spiritual courage—the kind of courage that "destroys giddiness at abysses" (Nietzsche 1988: 177) and responds instead with creativity.

"At-homeness in Being," in this more subtle sense of a proper orientation to Being and hence to our essential homelessness, can thus be "restored" by returning courageously to and facing the *unheimlich* explicitly—returning, that is, to the creative same-saying of language and hence to the nothing, to the advent of Being—again and again.

What is the state of dwelling in our precarious age? ... The proper plight of dwelling lies in this, that mortals ever search anew for the essence of dwelling, that *they must ever learn to dwell*. What if man's homelessness consisted in this, that man still does not even think of the *proper* plight of dwelling as *the* plight? Yet as soon as man *gives thought* to his homelessness, it is a misery no longer. Rightly considered and kept well in mind, it is the sole summons that *calls* mortals into their dwelling.

(Heidegger 1954: 363; original italics)

Giving thought to our essential homelessness involves waking and turning to face explicitly, and dwelling on, the *unheimlich* advent and adventure of being at all. This waking and turning is the original transformative achievement of education and the standing task of philosophical thinking, which tends to remain hidden because it is always before us.

Transcendence *Unheimlich*: The Shape of an Untiring Universality

I have been arguing that being at home in the world, a way of talking about the monumental ideals of education, is thoroughly *unheimlich*: to use the phrasing of Chapter 4, its achievement is the transcendental origin of an impossible aim. This means the basic character of our being at home in the world is exactly not that, insofar as we are always on the threshold of it, of standing in Being's midst by being held out into the nothing. Nietzsche says it well: "Man is a rope ... over an abyss" (1988: 43). There ought to be countless other ways of imagining the *unheimlich* character of our being held out into the nothing by living in language. That seems true insofar as language's creativity, which turns up everywhere and always partakes of and predicates on Being, is infinite. The question is what we can allow ourselves to imagine, and what is worth doing so. "There is nothing that is fundamentally excluded from being said," writes Gadamer: "Our capacity for saying keeps pace untiringly with the universality of reason" (1966a: 67).

I devote the rest of this chapter to suggesting that a phenomenological shape is discernible in this "untiring universality." The shape emerges when we bring together two of the main ideas of the foregoing chapters: (I) our standing, as metaphysical beings who transcend by thinking, always in the midst of Being; and (II) the endless turning and returning transformatively to itself of historical language, in which we live and think. These two insights, I believe, together represent the *unheimlich* symbiosis of permanence and flux, of presence and difference, or of sameness and change, that grants language its resilient meaningfulness and finite thinking its infinite reach. The resulting structure, which is essentially fluid and can be described as a phenomenological torus at the center of which stands every speaker of language, corresponds to the structure of educational ideals as I tried to explain it in Chapter 4: there is, first, the fundamental circumstance of education's transcendental achievements, such as rational freedom in the human individual; and second, the open question about what that might amount to conceptually and in practice—what it means, at all, to be a thinking being—with the resulting impossibility of fixing education's substantive aims. It also corresponds to the idea, modeled on the character of etymological understanding discussed in Chapter 3, that philosophical insight can give us the "true sense" of things—locating us where we already are and always were by orienting us generally to the historically incomplete whole of language in its unfinished unfolding of Being. The structure corresponds, moreover, to the idea introduced in Chapter 2, that language is the repository of historical mind, a fountain for thought which at once shapes and is shaped by thinking—so that the monumental achievement of education is nothing less than the renewed possibility of education itself. Finally, it corresponds to Wittgenstein's metaphor, first mentioned in Chapter 1 to describe the way in which language takes care of itself—as a house that carries its own foundation-walls.

If we understand language in these various ways as an historical manifold which (I) everywhere speaks to its own unity and (II) through infinite diversity always renews its own health, this helps to shed further light on Heidegger's tautological insight: "Language speaks solely and solitarily with itself" (2008c: 397–8). Language can speak solely and solitarily with itself insofar as it is an incomplete whole whose fundamental character is transformative self-understanding. Language is historically and conceptually unending: it is always "on the way"—but back to itself, transformatively as language, the *unheimlich* house of Being. Its returning to "the same" is its constantly transcending itself, gathering itself together, and repositioning itself in Being's midst. We ourselves, though, already stand at the center of language insofar as we partake of the understanding that, through it, becomes available to us. We ourselves, thinking beings who think Being by thinking and speaking, constitute that self-understanding character of language: our dwelling in language and especially in its creativity is constitutive of its health. We ourselves live in language, and at the same time language lives through us, its speakers.

A Symbiosis of Language and Self

That is to begin to uncover a symbiotic relationship between self and language, and explaining it will help present the conceptual structure I am trying to apply to Heidegger's insight. Introduced to language and at the same time to the world and ourselves we are swept up, caught up in a "dynamic whole *sui generis* that embraces even the subjectivity of the one" (Gadamer 1962a: 53).[13] We are introduced to something that is itself an "already going concern" (McDowell 1994: 125), which in education we come to understand by learning how to partake of, commune with, participate in as individuals. Here again we are not masters of our own house—nobody is master—but are just on the threshold.

In this appears the one side of the symbiosis: language stands "beyond the self" as something that thinking can always continue to pursue.[14] It is available for us, in thinking, to "get over ourselves" by "climbing beyond ourselves" to the community of mind that language is; but we can do this only insofar as language already stands "before us" transcendentally, as a precondition of our education and hence of our thought, just as our own educators stand before us historically, as elders; and we can recognize such preconditions only insofar as we continue to return to the historical transcendence that is thinking *per se*. We can think about who we are and where we came from. To "climb beyond" in this way is to return from the nothing to the nothing: it is to return to an orientation to that which is greater than, and beyond, each of us as individual persons and over against which we are as nothing. It is to return to a deep communion with other language speakers, minded beings who live in time and whose basic orientation is to reality at large.

> For what is more unconscious and "selfless" than that mysterious realm of language in which we stand and which allows what is to come to expression, so that being "is temporalized"? ... To put it in purely formal terms, the primacy that language and understanding have in Heidegger's thought indicates the priority of the "relation" over against its relational members—the I who understands and that which is understood. ... I believe that understanding involves a moment of "loss of self."
>
> (Gadamer 1962a: 50–1)

When we understand language we partake of something that is prior, greater, beyond. We partake of understanding itself—Being stood-in-the-midst-of. Right here in the midst of Being do we "lose ourselves" by partaking in a togetherness that already exists between understander and understood. That togetherness is the untiring universality of language and the great beyond of metaphysics, in which things come to stand out for us. Here in language we live and make our *unheimlich* home—as nothing, in the nothing. To climb beyond ourselves to language is to transcend ourselves by thinking "transcendentally," and that in turn is to partake explicitly in Being, "the transcendens pure and simple." "Hence language is ... the realm of human being-together, the realm of common understanding, of ever-replenished common agreement—a realm as indispensible to life as the air we breath" (Gadamer 1966a: 68).

In language we lose ourselves by partaking in universality as such; but already we can see, as with our at-homeness in Being, that this "moment of loss of self" is also the moment of its advent. It is precisely when we transcend ourselves by climbing beyond ourselves that we harken to Nietzsche's teaching: "Become what you are!" (1998: 252) McDowell writes in an appendix to *Mind and World* that language "stands over against all parties to communication in it, with a kind of independence of each of them that belongs with its meriting a kind of respect" (1994: 184)—namely, "the respect that is due to something to which we owe our being what we are" (184, n. 3). This latter bit—"our being what we are"—is the second part of the symbiosis I am sketching between language and self. McDowell is not doubting our free individuality: he is saying language stands beyond the self as a precondition of it. I argued in Chapter 4 that "what we are" is an open question; but we are that because we are thinking beings put into question by our own questioning. We can become what we are because we can transcend ourselves and imagine for ourselves what we might become. Our being caught up in the fount of historical mind is our becoming thinking beings at all, and that means rationally free individuals who must decide for ourselves how to live.

The priority of language need not be, and is not, the impersonal priority of some impregnable force raging across time and space, a great hive mind that we can only inhabit as passive, unthinking drones. On the contrary, language is available as a whole field of interpretation and creativity for its individual speakers, who enjoy in a great variety of ways the personal freedom that is distinctive of human being. As I argued in Chapter 3, only through individual acts of creative living and thinking does language exist as the great store of conceptual riches that it is. The "prior unity" of language is not only the precondition but also the consequence of its own historical diversity, whose furrows and folds we cultivate continuously by partaking in it as individuals. "Language," writes Gadamer, "is not the finally found anonymous subject of all social-historical processes and action" (1967b: 33). True, "[a]s Heidegger says, language speaks *us*, insofar as we do not really preside over it and control it"; but "no one disputes the fact that it is we who speak it" (1967a: 236; original italics).

That is a symbiosis, and it too can be described as *unheimlich*. It is *unheimlich* because, like so many of the philosophical insights I have been recommending in these chapters, it is a union of opposites whose character is healthy transformation. I have suggested that those insights can transform creatively for us the whole of language by saying nothing and everything at the same time. My suggesting further that we humans, all of us personally, stand at the center of a kind of conceptual torus—the fountain of language in flux, of historical mind speaking solely and solitarily with itself—is meant to give shape to this idea.

Transcendence *Unheimlich*: A Deep Common Accord

A torus—more or less a halo or ring in three dimensional space—is geometrically distinctive in that its "inner" and "outer" boundaries are on the same curved plane, so that to go in the direction of the one is to travel in a circle and so eventually to arrive back at the other. Natural examples include mushroom clouds and bubble rings, toroidal shapes whose dynamic flow pattern is the vortex. To try to recognize this shape and pattern in language and to maintain that we stand at the center of it is just to add historicity to the following insight from the *Tractatus*: "Contradiction, one might say, vanishes outside all propositions: tautology vanishes inside them. / Contradiction is the outer limit of propositions: tautology is the unsubstantial point at their centre" (2007: §5.143). Wittgenstein's thought here is that contradiction is what language everywhere denies: there stands its conceptual outer limit—the outlying boundary of meaningful language. By contrast, tautology is just language's inlying boundary, its same-saying, the common agreement affirmed everywhere in all thinking and speech. One such inner limit or unsubstantial central point Wittgenstein calls the "metaphysical subject," the first personal "I" implied everywhere by language and the "world" with which it is "one" (§§5.62–5.6331). Gadamer says something almost identical to this when he describes language as a "'reflection' of our own and all being," and as "the game of interpretation that we are all engaged in every day. In this game nobody is above and before all others; everybody is at the centre, is 'it' in this game. Thus it is always his turn to be interpreting" (1967b: 32). If we take these suggestions to heart, we might say that language has a shape, the tautological center of which is the thinking being, the understander who stands-in-the-midst.

What we can add to this shape is an emphasis on the historical nature of language—its ceaseless flow—the sense in which we must always be interpreting it and the world in which we live. We can emphasize its returning endlessly and transformatively to itself, the way it is always becoming different whenever we partake of it by thinking and speaking. That would be to emphasize the incompleteness of an incomplete whole, whose conceptual limits remain in suspension.

From an historical standpoint, those limits—what is called "tautology" and "contradiction," respectively—are not absolutely beyond question or just empty of meaning. An ordinary conversation is hardly void of general truths or risked absurdities: a balance of these keeps a conversation on the right path and in tune with itself. In fact making explicit, and revaluing, a host of such statements is the natural matter and mark of a good conversation. In that case we are liable to find that something we thought to be a mere contradiction or a mundane truth is not that, or not in the way we had imagined. It then becomes appropriate to avoid arrogance, say, by recognizing what strikes us as contradictory as yet another encounter with "the strange"—"something odd and unintelligible," "alien," "absurd"—but which might yet be "seen through" and "brought … into our linguistic world" (Gadamer 1967b: 32–3). It is also available for us to understand some apparent platitude again and anew in its affirmation of "the same," as I argued at the beginning of this chapter. There tautology fulfills the "constantly self-renewing contemporaneousness" of "all human experience of the world" (19) by reminding us of and reaffirming the togetherness and universality in which we partake every day.

An expressly historical view of language such as this has tautology and contradiction, inner and outer, suspended in a symbiotic relationship of mutual tension and support:

> Misunderstanding and strangeness are not the first factors, so that avoiding misunderstanding can be regarded as the specific task of hermeneutics. Just the reverse is the case. Only the support of familiar and common understanding makes possible the venture into the alien, the lifting up of something out of the alien, and thus the broadening and enrichment of our own experience of the world.
>
> (Gadamer 1966b: 15)

"Venturing into and lifting up out of the alien" means climbing beyond ourselves by bringing to explicit thought just that which seems to vanish at the limits of what we take to be meaningful. Language supports such adventurousness exactly by way of our "familiar and common understanding"—the relational priority of what we can call the same-saying of language, its true sense—that out and into which education leads us and according to which philosophy attempts to keep us centered. Venturing out into the alien, "we are possessed by something and precisely by means of it we are opened up for the new, the different, the true" (11).

That is what Gadamer means when he writes that every misunderstanding presupposes a "deep common accord" (1966b: 7). In misunderstanding something we already share in a universal togetherness with whatever is misunderstood; and that togetherness, that loss of self, is exactly the basis for our arriving at new understanding. In our encounter with the alien we do not know quite what to say about something or how to find our way about in it; but there is nothing strange that does not already betray a hint of familiarity insofar as we recognize it as something at all—even as something that we do not understand. This already presents the possibility of a better understanding of the thing and of arriving at a more enlightening way of speaking about it. It becomes interesting to us as a possible object of thought, and we might even call something "strange" with this meaning in mind. What a coincidence, then, that the word "interest" is just the conjunction of the Latin prefix *inter* (between, in the midst of) with the verb *esse* (to be). To recognize something as "strange" is already to find ourselves "standing-in-the-midst-of" what we do not understand; and just by this *unheimlich* combination of understanding and not understanding, of being-in and not being-in, are we "possessed" and our interests awakened to what is new and different and true.

In the case of another person the ideal result of this awakening is called "mutual understanding," being "at one" with respect to something: it is a "fusing of horizons" (Gadamer 2004b: 306) at the center of which each of us always stands, does not yet stand, is always coming to a stand. When we understand one another we each come to stand in the other's midst. We are "in" one another; we "know" each other. We then find that the "deep common accord," that center to which we return, has already been transformed for us, so that what was alien has become familiar, and what was familiar has become alien. We ourselves stand transformed with renewed understanding insofar as we apprehend the world and ourselves in a new way. We have been educated again, exposed again, led further out into the universe and reintroduced to ourselves. So transformed, we lose ourselves and gain ourselves at the same time. We become what we are.

Our sharing fundamentally in this deep common accord or universal togetherness suggests the whole world and everything in it is transcendentally interesting. Certainly it means reality, even at its most strange, should not be thought of "as lying beyond 'an outer boundary that encloses the conceptual sphere,'" as Bakhurst, citing McDowell, warns us against thinking (2011: 114; cf. McDowell 1994: 26). Exactly not: everything is interesting because it is already part of reality, with which we are always coming to terms by way of the untiring universality of language. It always remains available for us, whenever we encounter something that appears foreign or absurd or contradictory, to climb beyond ourselves to a better understanding of what the thing itself "says"—because we have already begun to do so, being already on the threshold of understanding. That is something of the constant "carrying over" in resilient language of what is already understood to whatever we do not yet understand. Thanks to language's untiring universality, even the greatest strangeness, diversity, or difference always confirms in no uncertain terms the absolute unity of reality.

Conclusion

What this spells is a word not quite uttered. It spells an endless circulation of unfinished language, where "every word breaks forth as from a center" (Gadamer 2004b: 454), from inner to outer and back around, through and through, again and again: it traces and then retraces the boundaries of a conceptual space always shaped afresh and creatively by the *unheimlich* symbiosis of alien and familiar, contradiction and tautology, unspoken and spoken, homelessness and at-homeness, misunderstanding and understanding, so that "every word, as the event of a moment, carries with it the unsaid, to which it is related by responding and summoning" (454). I have suggested it is possible to imagine this as the toroidal shape of language speaking solely and solitarily with itself—a kind of infinitely kaleidoscoping conceptual mandala. The benefit of such imagining is it helps us to hear language speaking, so that we can harken to what it says, so that we can answer its call.

I claim education and philosophy together are unique in that they harken to language's self-speech. They manifest the endless but unavoidable coming to terms with reality that constitutes the self-fulfilling activity of mind. The activities of education and philosophy continue to teach thinking insofar as they bring us ever into language and remind us ever of the deep common accord of which everything partakes by existing at all, and of which our knowing and speaking fulfills our historical transcendence as thinking beings.

Notes

1 "Even the Cartesian meditator, one supposes, anticipates that someone is listening to its otherwise private ratiocinations. Descartes himself was after all not only a thinker but an author and a highly skilled rhetorician—so skilled in fact as to lead us at times to forget a few elementary particulars about the very project of thought in which he was engaged. Even the *Meditations*, that quintessentially modern tribute to pure reason, was no private soliloquy but a literary work written and published with the anticipation that someone might read it and respond with a reasoned argument. That the reader responds is just as vital to the project as whether Descartes has hit upon the truth or beheld a clear and distinct idea" (Fairfield 2016: 127).

2 Cf. Gadamer (2004b: 385): "All this shows that a conversation has a spirit of its own, and that the language in which it is conducted bears its own truth within it—i.e., that it allows something to 'emerge' which henceforth exists."

3 "Language's rough ground" is the title of Chapter 2 of Standish's *Beyond the Self* (1992). He prefaces that chapter with the aphorism just cited: "We have got on to slippery ice where there is no friction and so in a certain sense the conditions are ideal, but also, just because of that, we are unable to walk. We want to walk: so we need friction. Back to the rough ground!"

4 Compare Cavell: "So what we are to know, or put together, in philosophy is what it is we (always already) know" (2012b: 208).

5 "A learning experience, or indeed any experience that is worthy of the name, leaves its subject in an important respect changed" (Fairfield 2009: 37).

6 Cf. Nietzsche (1997: §146): "He who fights with monsters should be careful lest he thereby become a monster. And if thou gaze long into an abyss, the abyss will also gaze into thee."

7 Compare (Bakhurst 2011: 159): "We might depict him [i.e., someone "'not at home' in some situation"] as 'not knowing his way around', as not knowing what to think, unable to grasp how to behave, ill at ease, anxious and confused, or at odds with himself."

8 Latin *pudendum* means "thing to be ashamed of." Freud quotes a dictionary: "*Heimlich* parts of the human body, *pudenda* ... 'the men that died were not smitten on their *heimlich* parts' (I Samuel 5:12)" (1919: 420).

9 The French is telling: the question "Qu'est-ce que tu veux dire?" means "What do you mean?"—but it translates literally to "What do you want to say?"

10 "I suddenly woke up in the midst of this dream, but only to the consciousness that I am dreaming and that I must go on dreaming lest I perish" (Nietzsche 1974: §54). "Where do we find ourselves? In a series of which we do not know the extremes, and believe that it has none. We wake and find ourselves on a stair; there are stairs

below us, which we seem to have ascended; there are stairs above us, many a one, which go upward and out of sight" (Emerson 1983: 3).
11 Cf. Nietzsche (1974: 32–8).
12 Cf. Gadamer (1963: 177): "Should it not be necessary, however, to define the business of philosophy, and the doctrine of language too, less negatively? In the last analysis, are not the concepts of ... language as an 'activity' or as a 'life form', for their part in need of 'healing', as Wittgenstein says?"
13 *Sui generis* means "of its own kind," so that it cannot be reduced to, or explained away by, some other concept: it must be understood from the inside.
14 This is one of Standish's fundamental points in *Beyond the Self* (1992).

Coda: Waking Thinking Being

In these chapters, I have been exploring the fundamental achievements of education and the deep connection that holds between education and philosophy. This has required a philosophical investigation of education, metaphysics, language, and reason in a way that respects their historical nature. It has also required a renewed attention to the nature of philosophical thinking. In these final remarks I extend my recent, frantic speculations by emphasizing the sheer universality to which education introduces us. I suggest that if we can accept our own thinking transcendentally as the *unheimlich* speech of historical language, which thinks Being by standing in its very midst, then perhaps we can say, even further, that education is waking Being itself to its own thinking.

The *unheimlich* character of our transcending in language by harkening to it is hardly more evident than when the self-directed, tautological sayings of philosophy begin to toy with contradiction. Consider the following moments of philosophical thinking:

> I sought myself. (Heraclitus: fr. 101; cf. Diels and Kranz 1985)
> I know that I know nothing. (cf. Plato 1966: 21d)[1]
> Know thyself. (cf. Plato 1925: 229e)
> I am, I exist. (Descartes 2008: 19)
> Become what you are! (Nietzsche 1988: 252)
> Whatever we cannot speak of we must pass over in silence. (Wittgenstein 2007: §7)
> Man is condemned to be free. (Sartre 2007: 29)
> Most thought-provoking for our thought-provoking time is that we are still not thinking. (Heidegger 1968: 370–1)

In each of these purported tautologies there is not only an air of paradox, verging on absurdity or meaninglessness: more than that, each saying acknowledges that the basic unity of the speaker—the metaphysical I, the thinking being—has been put into question; and yet with each saying the speaker turns and faces that nihilation explicitly, in a creative attempt to climb beyond it to fresher heights and richer depths.

Returning to a discussion first breached in this book's overture, I suppose this is how we might reinterpret the notion of "that inarticulate sound with which many writers would like to begin philosophy," whose aim according to Wittgenstein is to "begin before the beginning" (1975: §68). We might say rather that the aim, impossible in itself, is to arrive at an ever new beginning by embracing again and again the whole of reality and experience in a single phrase, by saying everything at the same time—like uttering the name of God, or declaring with Nietzsche that "*God is dead!*" (1974: §125; 1988: §2; italics in the latter). We might say the subsequent "inarticulate sound"—I imagine something really inarticulate, an immutable shriek of terrified exhilaration, like "*Manmbistdmalntk?!*"—reflects, in "the event of a moment" (Gadamer 2004b: 454), the sheer impossibility of this total saying, while still wanting to carry with it the force of everything that remains unsaid—the incomplete whole of language. It seems only language speakers, idiots, beings not-at-home, who philosophize by nature and transcend by thinking, can dream of such a saying.

Perhaps the "inarticulate sound" of philosophical thinking breaking out in this way, its "nothing-saying," aspires to tautology as much as any of its more studied sayings, and not in an insignificant or even unhelpful way, since we can recognize its inarticulate character as a performance of that same self-effacement. Articulate and not, understood and not, these human sayings speak profoundly of the experience of utter incompleteness, of something left unarticulated and inarticulate—the self-knowing of historical finitude. Again, however, from this we need not acquiesce in the silence of the *Tractatus*: on the contrary, perhaps these inarticulate sounds represent the growing pains of historical mind. The daring performance of saying something we have deemed unspeakable reflects the only dimension in which this *unheimlich* transformation of meaning-in-the-midst can possibly occur: the historical dimension. There the saying comes into its own as an incomplete whole, a voicing of our ever-lengthening call for more understanding, more questioning, more saying. It becomes a wholehearted affirmation of its own incompleteness and the incompleteness of all life and growth. That dimension, again, is the creative beyond of metaphysics, of language unfolding Being in time. The aspiring character of philosophy's saying, never quite articulate, is perhaps itself the possibility of creativity, of healthy transformation through historical transcendence. It is perhaps language always on the way back to itself, returning to its own speech and centering itself again on the universality and fundamental togetherness Being, our unknown home. What that spells is the inevitable possibility of learning.

I offer a final suggestion about the phenomenological shape of language. I must emphasize the sense in which our being minded entails our standing, and always coming to stand, at the center of the conceptual space that language presents. Language is not some "thing" that is "over there," but the "clearing-concealing advent of Being itself" (Heidegger 1947: 230). It would be a mistake to see language first as some imaginary object—whose shape for us has been a torus, a fountain that is its own source—existing in some imaginary space, which we could then theorize about from the outside. We should rather understand language itself as the preeminent space, that first beyond in which things stand out and at whose center we ourselves, the beginnings and endings of language, stand.

Recall that education is philosophical in nature insofar as philosophy is thinking about things in general from the inside of things in general. We humans are thinking from the inside of things insofar as we stand, each of us personally, at the center of that space unfolded by language. Compare Bakhurst's commentary on what he calls "the character of the space of reasons":

> The *idée fixe* is that the topography of the space of reasons must be appreciated from within, and not theorized from some philosophical vantage point. Yet accepting all this does not preclude sustained speculative reflection on our practices from within, reflection aimed to deepen our appreciation of their nature. Such reflection might yield an array of concepts that enable us to attain critical distance from our subject matter without casting it from sideways-on.
>
> (2011: 102)

It is exactly "from within" the space unfolded by language that we can think about that space: only from here, within ourselves, can we attain critical distance from ourselves, so that we stand out to ourselves as an object of thought. The difficulty of philosophical reflection, as Wittgenstein knew early on, is that we can see the limits of our thinking only from within those limits. What he did not want explicitly to acknowledge, for fear of speaking nonsense, is our standing task of finding the creativity and courage to transcend those limits exactly by confronting and apprehending the unspeakable. A mere child brings us to the edge of the abyss by constantly asking, "Why?" She can, in the end, only be answered half-jokingly with some half-articulate reassurance; but so must we seek that abyss from within in order to say what has not been and even cannot be said. It is precisely when we dare to give voice to the unspeakable that we become what we are.

For example, something that might be unspeakable, but which we might yet dare to say, is that we ourselves are that reality, that "things-in-general"—from the inside of which and about which we, beings who think, are thinking.

Wittgenstein writes, "There are two godheads: the world and my independent I" (1961: 74). On the other hand, "I am my world" (2007: §5.63). If that is solipsism—intellectual masturbation at its finest, perhaps, the belief that there is only one mind and that it belongs only to the one thinking—then suppose it is a healthy one. Suppose it is a solipsism that, as Wittgenstein puts it, "coincides with pure realism. The self of solipsism shrinks to a point without extension, and there remains the reality co-ordinated with it" (§5.64). That too, Wittgenstein supposes, would coincide with idealism, the view that mind and reality are one:

> This is the way I have travelled: Idealism singles out men from the world as unique, solipsism singles me alone out, and at last I see that I too belong with the rest of the world, and so on the one side *nothing* is left over, and on the other side, as unique, *the world*. In this way idealism leads to realism if it is strictly thought out.
>
> (1961: 85; original italics)

Gadamer describes these thoughts as "obsolete-sounding": "'The subject does not belong to the world: rather, it is a limit of the world,' or better, its presupposition. This is all very unclear and sounds like Schopenhauer. It is no less unclear how Wittgenstein intends to go from idealism via solipsism to realism" (1963: 174). What Wittgenstein means, I think, is just that a healthy solipsism, a relaxed idealism, and a common sense realism are all good insights into, and ways of talking about, the same world in which we all live as thinking beings.[2] As McDowell puts it, "Any idealism with a chance of being credible must aspire to being such that, if thought through, it stands revealed as fully cohering with the realism of common sense" (2009a: 141).[3] To take the insights together is just to make explicit the variety of ways of understanding that togetherness, that deep common accord, in which we all partake by thinking and being. The "one thinking" of solipsism is the "one thinking" of idealism, and that is the "one thinking" of realism. Reality itself is the one thinking. If it were something like Hegel's "Absolute Knowing" (cf. Hegel 1977: C.DD), then Gadamer's answer would lie in his own words: "No one knew better than did German idealism that consciousness and its object are not two separated worlds" (1962b: 119). Coming to terms with reality means coming to terms with the oneness with reality that each of personally enjoys, and that we all enjoy together.

It is possible to apply this shape—that is, the symbiotic coinciding of inside and outside, of "the two godheads, the world and my independent I"—to the notion of mindedness as standing in the midst of Being. We can identify with language insofar as we are its own self-understanding character, the understander who harkens to language's self-speech. Language in turn identifies with Being insofar as it is Being that can be stood-in-the-midst-of. If we, as thinking beings, partake in Being by existing at all, and if we think Being by standing in its very midst, then wherever beings are thinking, there is Being thinking Being. Our ability to think transcendentally implies that we partake in the *"the transcendens pure and simple"* (Heidegger 1927: 85; original italics and stylization) by thinking it, and that we can recognize our so partaking in the fact of our existing at all; but this also means Being, the transcendens itself, is fundamentally what does the transcending. In thinking, Being transcends itself: it thinks itself by way of beings that think.

What might be unspeakable, but which we might yet dare to say, is that in education we wake to thinking Being; but we also wake Being itself to its own thinking by introducing it to itself—to language, Being already stood-in-the-midst-of. In other words, in education the universe turns itself inside out. The self-consciousness of the human turns out to be the self-consciousness of Being, the unifying principle of what is. Can we find it within ourselves to come to terms with this? It would mean coming to terms with the idea that through education, the historical leading out and into the midst, reality itself comes to know itself, by waking and turning toward, and dwelling on, its own advent—a metaphysical achievement. I believe we can aspire in education and in philosophy to this waking and this turning toward, and coming to terms with, the self-identity of reality. We can aspire to a becoming reality that knows itself, speaks with itself, educates itself, cares for itself—and imagines for itself its own destiny.

That might be like arriving endlessly at the beginning of thinking. It might be like living in a home that carries its own foundation walls. It might be like waking thinking Being.

Notes

1   Although this phrasing does not appear anywhere in Plato's works, it is attributed to, and at least derivable from, Socrates's philosophy. Diogenes Laërtius writes of Socrates: "He used to say … that he knew nothing except just the fact of his ignorance" (1972: II.5.32).
2   This at once mutually exclusive and transposable trifecta of metaphysical insights point to a possible criticism of my apprehending language as a torus insofar as that shape represents, mathematically, an orientable surface. There is perhaps

an important sense in which language is a non-orientable manifold, as is the Möbius strip or the Roman surface. My speculative description of transformative understanding is meant to shed light on that sense, but it may be that a more complex structure than the torus is in order.

3   In a footnote, McDowell cites those passages from the *Tractatus* and the *Notebooks* that I have just cited, adding, "[T]he coincidence with realism is directly credited to solipsism, which figures in the route from idealism to realism in the *Notebooks*" (141, n. 17).

References

Allen, G. (1894), *Post-Prandial Philosophy*, London: Chatto and Windus.

Aristotle (1931), *The Works of Aristotle: De Anima*, trans. J. A. Smith, Oxford: Clarendon Press.

Aristotle (1995), *The Complete Works of Aristotle: The Revised Oxford Translation*, ed. J. Barnes, Princeton: Princeton University Press.

Axelrod, P., P. Anisef, and Z. Lin (2001), "Against All Odds? The Enduring Value of Liberal Education in Universities, Professions, and the Labour Market," *The Canadian Journal of Higher Education*, 31 (2): 47–78.

Baggs, A. [silentmiaow] (2007), "In My Language," YouTube, January 14. Available online: https://www.youtube.com/watch?v=JnylM1hI2jc (accessed July 2020).

Bakhurst, D. (2005), "Ilyenkov on Education," *Studies in Past European Thought*, 57 (3): 261–75.

Bakhurst, D. (2011), *The Formation of Reason*, Malden, MA: Wiley-Blackwell.

Bakhurst, D. (2012), "Freedom and Second Nature in the Formation of Reason," *Mind, Culture, and Activity*, 19 (2): 172–89.

Bakhurst, D. (2014), "Training, Transformation and Education," *Royal Institute of Philosophy Supplement*, 76: 301–27.

Bakhurst, D. (2015), "Understanding Vygotsky," *Learning, Culture and Social Interaction*, 5: 1–4.

Bakhurst, D. (2016a), "Introduction: Exploring the Formation of Reason," *Journal of Philosophy of Education*, 50 (1): 76–83.

Bakhurst, D. (2016b), "Response to Rödl, Standish and Derry," *Journal of Philosophy of Education*, 50 (1): 123–9.

Bakhurst, D. (2018), "Activity, Action and Self-consciousness," *Educational Review*, 70 (1): 91–9.

Bakhurst, D. and P. Fairfield, eds. (2016), *Education and Conversation: Exploring Oakeshott's Legacy*, London: Bloomsbury.

Barnhart, R. K. (1988), *The Barnhart Dictionary of Etymology*, Hackensack, NJ: H. W. Wilson).

Barrow, R. and P. White, eds. (1993), *Beyond Liberal Education: Essays in Honour of Paul H. Hirst*, Oxford: Routledge.

Beiser, F. C. (1998), "A Romantic Education: The Concept of *Bildung* in Early German Romanticism," in A. O. Rorty (ed.), *Philosophers on Education*, 284–99, New York: Routledge.

Bermudez, J. L. (2006), "Animal Reasoning and Proto-Logic," in S. Hurley and M. Nudds (eds.), *Rational Animals?*, 127–38, Oxford: Oxford University Press.

Bernstein, R. J. (2008), "The Conversation That Never Happened (Gadamer/Derrida)," *The Review of Metaphysics*, 61 (3): 577–603.

Blake, N., P. Smeyers, R. Smith, and P. Standish. (2000), *Education in an Age of Nihilism: Education and Moral Standards*, Oxford: Routledge.

Blake, N., P. Smeyers, R. Smith, and P. Standish, eds. (2003), *The Blackwell Guide to the Philosophy of Education*, Malden, MA: Blackwell.

Buck, C. D. (2008), *A Dictionary of Selected Synonyms in the Principal Indo-European Languages*, Chicago: University of Chicago Press.

Cahn, S., ed. (2009), *Philosophy of Education: The Essential Texts*, New York: Routledge.

Callahan, R. E. (1962), *Education and the Cult of Efficiency*, London: University of Chicago Press.

Canada (2012), "Advisory Panel on Canada's International Education Strategy," in *International Education: A Key Driver of Canada's Future Prosperity*, Ottawa: Minister of International Trade.

Candland, D. K. (1993), *Feral Children and Clever Animals*, New York: Oxford University Press.

Carr, D. (1999), "Rational Curriculum Planning: In Pursuit of an Illusion," in R. Marples (ed.), *The Aims of Education*, 173–84, London: Routledge.

Cavell, S. (1979), *The Claim of Reason*, New York: Oxford University Press.

Cavell, S. (2012a), "Philosophy as the Education of Grownups," in N. Saito and P. Standish (eds.), *Stanley Cavell and the Education of Grownups*, 19–32, New York: Fordham University Press.

Cavell, S. (2012b), "Philosophy as Education," in N. Saito and P. Standish (eds.), *Stanley Cavell and the Education of Grownups*, 207–13, New York: Fordham University Press.

Cohen, S. M. (2020), "Aristotle's Metaphysics," *Stanford Encyclopedia of Philosophy*. Available online: https://plato.stanford.edu/entries/aristotle-metaphysics/ (accessed July 2020).

Conant, J. and C. Diamond (2004), "On Reading the *Tractatus* Resolutely: Reply to Meredith Williams and Peter Sullivan," in M. Kölbel and B. Weiss (eds.), *Wittgenstein's Lasting Significance*, 46–99, New York: Routledge.

Conroy, J., R. Davis, and P. Enslin (2008), "Philosophy as a Basis for Policy and Practice: What Confidence Can We Have in Philosophical Analysis and Argument?" *Journal of Philosophy of Education*, 42 (1): 165–82.

Council of Europe (2001), *Report from the Educational Council to the European Council on the Concrete Future Objectives of Education and Training Systems* (5980/01).

Curren, R., ed. (2008), *A Companion to the Philosophy of Education*, Malden, MA: Blackwell.

Cuypers, S. (2014a), "John White's Radically Practical Conception of Educational Philosophy: An Assessment," *Papers 2014 Philosophy of Education Society of Great Britain Oxford Conference*.

Cuypers, S. (2014b), "The Power and Limits of Philosophy of Education," *Theory and Research in Education*, 12 (1): 54–64.

Davidson, D. (1974), "On the Very Idea of a Conceptual Scheme," *Proceedings and Addresses of the American Philosophical Association*, 47: 5–20.

Davidson, D. (1986), "A Nice Derangement of Epitaphs," in Davidson, *Truth, Language, and History*, 89–108, Oxford: Oxford University Press.

Davidson, D. (2005), *Truth, Language, and History*, Oxford: Oxford University Press.

Davis, A. (1998), *The Limits of Educational Assessment*, Malden, MA: Blackwell.

Davis, A. (2009), "Examples as Method? My Attempts to Understand Assessment and Fairness (in the Spirit of the Later Wittgenstein)," *Journal of Philosophy of Education*, 43 (3): 371–89.

Davis, A. (2013), "How Far Can We Aspire to Consistency When Assessing Learning?" *Ethics and Education*, 8 (3): 217–28.

Davis, A. (2014), "Reading Lessons: Why Synthetic Phonics Doesn't Work," *The Guardian*, March 4. Available online: http://www.theguardian.com/teacher-network/teacher-blog/2014/mar/04/reading-lessons-phonics-world-book-day (accessed July 2020).

Davis, R. A (2011), "Brilliance of a Fire: Innocence, Experience and the Theory of Childhood," *Journal of Philosophy of Education*, 45 (2): 379–97.

Dearden, R. (1972), "Autonomy and Education," in R. Dearden, P. H. Hirst, and R. S. Peters (eds.), *Education and the Development of Reason*, 448–65, Routledge and Kegan Paul: London.

De Caro, M. and D. Macarthur, eds. (2004), *Naturalism in Question*, Cambridge, MA: Harvard University Press.

Dennett, D. (1995) "Do Animals Have Beliefs?" in H. Roitblat and J. A. Meyer (eds.), *Comparative Approaches to Cognitive Science*, 111–18, Cambridge, MA: MIT Press.

Derrida, J. (2004), "Différance," in J. Rivkin and M. Ryan (eds.), *Literary Theory: An Anthology*, 278–99, Oxford: Blackwell.

Derry, J. (2008), "Abstract Rationality in Education: From Vygotsky to Brandom," *Studies in Philosophy and Education*, 27: 49–62.

Derry, J. (2013), *Vygostky: Philosophy and Education*, Malden, MA: Wiley Blackwell.

Descartes, R. (2008), *Meditations on First Philosophy*, Oxford: Oxford University Press.

Diels, H. and W. Kranz, eds. (1985), *Die Fragmente der Vorsokratiker*, Zurich: Weidmann.

Dretske, F. I. (2006), "Minimal Rationality," in S. Hurley and M. Nudds (eds.), *Rational Animals?*, 107–16, Oxford: Oxford University Press.

Du Bois, W. E. B. (1994), *The Souls of Black Folk*, Dover: New York.

Emerson, R. W. (1983), *The Collected Works of Ralph Waldo Emerson. Volume III, Essays: Second Series*, Cambridge, MA: Harvard University Press.

Fairfield, P. (2009), *Education after Dewey*, London: Continuum.

Fairfield, P. (2011), *Philosophical Hermeneutics Reinterpreted*, London: Continuum.

Fairfield, P. (2016), "A Phenomenology of Listening," in Bakhurst and Fairfield (eds.), *Education and Conversation: Exploring Oakeshott's Legacy*, 127–41, London: Bloomsbury.

Freud, S. (1919), "The Uncanny," in J. Rivkin and M. Ryan (eds.), *Literary Theory: An Anthology*, 418–30, Oxford: Blackwell.

Gadamer, H.-G. (1962a), "On the Problem of Self-Understanding," in H.-G. Gadamer (ed.), *Philosophical Hermeneutics*, 44–58, trans. D. E. Linge, Berkeley: University of California Press.

Gadamer, H.-G. (1962b), "The Philosophical Foundations of the Twentieth Century," in H.-G. Gadamer, *Philosophical Hermeneutics*, 107–29, trans. D. E. Linge, Berkeley: University of California Press.

Gadamer, H.-G. (1963), "The Phenomenological Movement," in H.-G. Gadamer, *Philosophical Hermeneutics*, 130–81, trans. D. E. Linge, Berkeley: University of California Press.

Gadamer, H.-G. (1966a), "Man and Language," in H.-G. Gadamer, *Philosophical Hermeneutics*, 59–68, trans. D. E. Linge, Berkeley: University of California Press.

Gadamer, H.-G. (1966b), "The Universality of the Hermeneutical Problem," in H.-G. Gadamer, *Philosophical Hermeneutics*, 3–17, trans. D. E. Linge, Berkeley: University of California Press.

Gadamer, H.-G. (1967a), "Heidegger and the Language of Metaphysics," in H.-G. Gadamer, *Philosophical Hermeneutics*, 229–40, trans. D. E. Linge, Berkeley: University of California Press.

Gadamer, H.-G. (1967b), "On the Scope and Function of Hermeneutical Reflection," in H.-G. Gadamer, *Philosophical Hermeneutics*, 18–43, trans. D. E. Linge, Berkeley: University of California Press.

Gadamer, H.-G. (1976), *Philosophical Hermeneutics*, trans. D. E. Linge, Berkeley: University of California Press.

Gadamer, H.-G. (2004a), "Supplement II: To What Extent Does Language Preform Thought?" in Gadamer, *Truth and Method*, 546–53, trans. J. Weinsheimer and D. G. Marshall, London: Continuum.

Gadamer, H.-G. (2004b), *Truth and Method*, trans. J. Weinsheimer and D. G. Marshall, London: Continuum.

Gingell, J. and C. Winch (2004), *Philosophy and Educational Policy: A Critical Introduction*, New York: RoutledgeFalmer.

Glock, H. J. (2000), "Animals, Thoughts, and Concepts," *Synthese*, 123: 35–64.

Glock, H. J. (2009), "Can Animals Act for Reasons?" *Inquiry*, 52: 232–54.

Glock, H. J. (2010), "Can Animals Judge?" *Dialectica*, 64: 11–33.

Grayling, A. C. (1996), *Wittgenstein: A Very Short Introduction*, Oxford: Oxford University Press.

Heidegger, M. (1927), "Being and Time: Introduction," in D. F. Krell (ed.), *Heidegger, Basic Writings*, 41–87, London: Harper.

Heidegger, M. (1929), "What Is Metaphysics?" in Heidegger, D. F. Krell (ed.), *Basic Writings*, 93–110, London: Harper.

Heidegger, M. (1947), "Letter on Humanism," in Heidegger, D. F. Krell (ed.), *Basic Writings*, 217–65, London: Harper.

Heidegger, M. (1954), "Building Dwelling Thinking," in Heidegger, D. F. Krell (ed.), *Basic Writings*, 347–63, London: Harper.

Heidegger, M. (1968), "What Calls for Thinking?" in Heidegger, D. F. Krell (ed.), *Basic Writings*, 369–91, London: Harper.

Heidegger, M. (1972), "The End of Philosophy and the Task of Thinking," in Heidegger, D. F. Krell (ed.), *Basic Writings*, 441–9, London: Harper.

Heidegger, M. (2008a), *Basic Writings*, ed. D. F. Krell, London: Harper.

Heidegger, M. (2008b), "On the Essence of Truth," in Heidegger, D. F. Krell (ed.), *Basic Writings*, 115–38, London: Harper.

Heidegger, M. (2008c), "The Way to Language," in Heidegger, D. F. Krell (ed.), *Basic Writings*, 397–426, London: Harper.

Hegel, G. W. F. (1977), *Phenomenology of Spirit*, Oxford: Oxford University Press.

Hirst, P. (1975), *Knowledge and the Curriculum*, London: Routledge and Kegan Paul.

Hirst, P. (1993), "Education, Knowledge and Practices," in R. Barrow and P. White (eds.), *Beyond Liberal Education: Essays in Honour of Paul H. Hirst*, 184–99, Oxford: Routledge.

Hirst, P. (1999), "The Nature of Educational Aims," in R. Marples (ed.), *The Aims of Education*, 124–32, London: Routledge.

Hoad, T. F., ed. (1996), *The Concise Oxford Dictionary of English Etymology*, Oxford: Oxford University Press.

Hogan, P. and R. Smith (2003), "Philosophy and the Practice of Education," in N. Blake, P. Smeyers, R. Smith, and P. Standish (eds.), *The Blackwell Guide to the Philosophy of Education*, 165–80, Malden, MA: Blackwell.

Hume, D. (2000), *A Treatise of Human Nature*, Oxford: Oxford University Press.

Hurley, S. and M. Nudds, eds. (2006), *Rational Animals?*, Oxford: Oxford University Press.

Kant, I. (1960), *Education*, trans. A. Churton, Ann Arbor: University of Michigan Press.

Kaufmann, W., ed. and trans. (1982), *The Portable Nietzsche*, New York: Penguin.

Klein, E. (1971), *A Comprehensive Etymological Dictionary of the English Language*, New York, Elsevier.

Kölbel, M. and B. Weiss, eds. (2010), *Wittgenstein's Lasting Significance*, New York: Routledge.

Kotzee, B., A. Carter, and H. Siegel (2019), "Educating for Intellectual Virtue: A Critique from Action Guidance," *Episteme*, 2019: 1–23.

Lane, H. (1976), *The Wild Boy of Aveyron*, Cambridge, MA: Harvard University Press.

Laërtius, D. (1972), *Lives of Eminent Philosophers*, trans. R. D. Hicks, Cambridge, MA: Harvard University Press.

Løvelie, L. and P. Standish (2002), "Introduction: *Bildung* and the Idea of a Liberal Education," *Journal of Philosophy of Education*, 36 (3): 317–40.

Lyotard, J.-F. (1984), *The Postmodern Condition: A Report on Knowledge*, trans. G. Bennington and B. Massumi, Minneapolis: University of Minnesota Press.

Malson, L. (1972), *Wolf Children*, trans. E. Fawcett, P. Ayrton, and J. White, London: Monthly Review Press.

Marples, R., ed. (1999), *The Aims of Education*, London: Routledge.

McDowell, J. (1994), *Mind and World*, Cambridge, MA: Harvard University Press.

McDowell, J. (2004), "Naturalism in the Philosophy of Mind," in M. De Caro and D. Macarthur (eds.), *Naturalism in Question*, 91–105, Cambridge, MA: Harvard University Press.

McDowell, J. (2009a), "Conceptual Capacities in Perception," in J. McDowell, (ed.), *Having the World in View*, 127–44, Cambridge, MA: Harvard University Press.

McDowell, J. (2009b), "Towards a Reading of Hegel on Action in the 'Reason' Chapter of the Phenomenology," in J. McDowell (ed.), *Having the World in View*, 166–84, Cambridge, MA: Harvard University Press.

McDowell, J. (2009c), *Having the World in View*, Cambridge, MA, Harvard University Press.

Milner, J. O., L. M. Milner, and J. F. Mitchell (2012), *Bridging English*, Boston: Pearson.

Nietzsche, F. (1873), "On Truth and Lie in an Extra-Moral Sense," in Kaufmann (ed. and trans.), *The Portable Nietzsche*, 42–6, New York: Penguin.

Nietzsche, F. (1967), *The Will to Power*, trans. W. Kaufmann, New York: Random House.

Nietzsche, F. (1974), *The Gay Science*, trans. W. Kaufmann, New York, Random House.

Nietzsche, F. (1988), *Thus Spoke Zarathustra*, trans. R. J. Hollingdale, London: Penguin.

Nietzsche, F. (1997), *Beyond Good and Evil*, trans. H. Zimmern, Mineola, NY: Dover.

Nussbaum, M. C. (2009), "Education for Profit, Education for Freedom," *Liberal Education*, 95 (3): 6–13.

Pavco-Giaccia, O., M. F. Little, J. Stanley, and Y. Dunham (2019), "Rationality Is Gendered," *Collabra: Psychology*, 5 (1): 1–15.

Peters, M. and K. Wain (2003), "Postmodernism/Post-structuralism," in N. Blake, P. Smeyers, R. Smith, and P. Standish (eds.), *The Blackwell Guide to the Philosophy of Education*, 57–72, Malden, MA: Blackwell.

Peters, R. S. (1975), "General Editor's Note," in Hirst, *Knowledge and the Curriculum*, vii–viii, London: Routledge and Kegan Paul.

Plato (1925), *Plato in Twelve Volumes*, vol. 9, trans. H. N. Fowler, Cambridge, MA: Harvard University Press.

Plato (1966), *Plato in Twelve Volumes*, vol. 1, trans. H. N. Fowler, Cambridge, MA: Harvard University Press.

Reznikoff, C. (2005), *The Poems of Charles Reznikoff: 1918–1975*, Boston, Black Sparrow.

Rivkin, J. and M. Ryan, eds. (2004), *Literary Theory: An Anthology*, Oxford: Blackwell.

Rödl, S. (2007), *Self-Consciousness*, London: Harvard University Press.

Rödl, S. (2016), "Education and Autonomy," *Journal of Philosophy of Education*, 50 (1): 84–97.

Rödl, S. (2020), "Teaching, Freedom and the Human Individual," *Journal of Philosophy of Education*, 54 (2): 290–304.

Roitblat, H. and J. A. Meyer, eds. (1995), *Comparative Approaches to Cognitive Science*, Cambridge, MA: MIT Press.

Rorty, A. O., ed. (1998), *Philosophers on Education*, New York: Routledge.
Rorty, R. (1979), *Philosophy and the Mirror of Nature*, Princeton: Princeton University Press.
Rorty, R. (1982), *Consequences of Pragmatism*, Minneapolis: University of Minnesota Press.
Rorty, R. (1983), "Pragmatism without Method," in R. Rorty (ed.), *Objectivity, Relativism, and Truth*, 63–77, Cambridge: Cambridge University Press.
Rorty, R. (1984), "The Historiography of Philosophy," in R. Rorty (ed.), *Truth and Progress*, 247–73, Cambridge: Cambridge University Press.
Rorty, R. (1985), "Texts and Lumps," in R. Rorty (ed.), *Objectivity, Relativism, and Truth*, 78–92, Cambridge: Cambridge University Press.
Rorty, R. (1988), "Representation, Social Practice, and Truth," in R. Rorty (ed.), *Objectivity, Relativism, and Truth*, 151–62, Cambridge, Cambridge University Press.
Rorty, R. (1989a), *Contingency, Irony, and Solidarity*, Cambridge: Cambridge University Press.
Rorty, R. (1989b), "Private Irony and Liberal Hope," in R. Rorty (ed.), *Contingency, Irony, and Solidarity*, 73–95, Cambridge: Cambridge University Press.
Rorty. R. (1989c), "The Contingency of Language," in R. Rorty (ed.), *Contingency, Irony, and Solidarity*, 3–22, Cambridge: Cambridge University Press.
Rorty, R. (1990), "The Dangers of Over-Philosophication—Reply to Arcilla and Nicholson," *Educational Theory*, 40 (1): 41–4.
Rorty, R. (1991a), *Essays on Heidegger and Others*, Cambridge: Cambridge University Press.
Rorty, R. (1991b), *Objectivity, Relativism, and Truth*, Cambridge: Cambridge University Press.
Rorty, R. (1991c), "Philosophy as Science, as Metaphor, and as Politics," in R. Rorty (ed.), *Essays on Heidegger and Others*, 9–26, Cambridge: Cambridge University Press.
Rorty, R. (1991d), "Wittgenstein, Heidegger and the Reification of Language," in R. Rorty (ed.), *Essays on Heidegger and Others*, 50–65, Cambridge: Cambridge University Press.
Rorty, R. (1998a), "The Very Idea of Human Answerability to the World: John McDowell's Version of Empiricism," in R. Rorty (ed.), *Truth and Progress*, 138–52, Cambridge: Cambridge University Press.
Rorty, R. (1998b), *Truth and Progress*, Cambridge: Cambridge University Press.
Rorty, R. (2007a), "Grandeur, Profundity, and Finitude," in R. Rorty (ed.), *Philosophy as Cultural Politics*, 73–88, Cambridge: Cambridge University Press.
Rorty, R. (2007b), *Philosophy as Cultural Politics*, Cambridge: Cambridge University Press.
Rorty, R. (2007c), "Wittgenstein and the Linguistic Turn," in R. Rorty (ed.), *Philosophy as Cultural Politics*, 160–75, Cambridge: Cambridge University Press.
Ross, W. D., trans. (1924), *Aristotle's Metaphysics: A Revised Text with Introduction and Commentary*, Oxford: Clarendon Press.

Ruitenberg, C. (2010), "Distance and Defamiliarization: Translation as Philosophical Method," in C. Ruitenberg (ed.), *What Do Philosophers of Education Do (And How Do They Do It?)*, 103–15, Malden, MA: Wiley-Blackwell.

Ruitenberg, C. (2010), *What Do Philosophers of Education Do (And How Do They Do It?)*, Malden, MA: Wiley-Blackwell.

Saito, N. and P. Standish, eds. (2012), *Stanley Cavell and the Education of Grownups*, New York: Fordham University Press.

Sartre, J. P. (2007), *Existentialism Is a Humanism*, trans. C. Macomber, London: Yale University Press.

Scheffler, I. (1970), "Philosophy and the Curriculum," in I. Scheffler (ed.), *Reason and Teaching*, 31–44, London: Routledge and Kegan Paul.

Scheffler, I. (1973), *Reason and Teaching*, London: Routledge and Kegan Paul.

Scheffler, I. (2009), *Worlds of Truth: A Philosophy of Knowledge*, Malden, MA: Wiley-Blackwell.

Sellars, W. (1963a), *Empiricism and the Philosophy of Mind*, London: Routledge and Kegan Paul Ltd.

Sellars, W. (1963b), "Philosophy and the Scientific Image of Man," in W. Sellars (ed.), *Empiricism and the Philosophy of Mind*, 1–40, London: Routledge and Kegan Paul Ltd.

Sheffler, I. (1964), "Philosophical Models of Teaching," in I. Scheffler (ed.), *Reason and Teaching*, 67–81, London: Routledge and Kegan Paul.

Siegel, H. (1988), *Educating Reason: Rationality, Critical Thinking, and Education*, New York: Routledge.

Siegel, H. (1996), *Rationality Redeemed? Further Dialogues on an Educational Ideal*, Routledge, New York.

Siegel, H. (2005), "Israel Scheffler Interviewed by Harvey Siegel," *Journal of Philosophy of Education*, 39 (4): 647–59.

Siegel, H. (2008), "Autonomy, Critical Thinking and the Wittgensteinian Legacy: Reflections on Christopher Winch, Education, Autonomy, and Critical Thinking," *Journal of Philosophy of Education*, 42 (1): 165–84.

Siegel, H. (2014), "Bildung, the Space of Reasons, and the Educational Aim of Autonomy," *Papers 2014 Philosophy of Education Society of Great Britain Oxford Conference*.

Siegel, H. (2017), *Education's Epistemology*, Oxford: Oxford University Press.

Smeyers, P., R. Smith, and P. Standish (2007), *The Therapy of Education: Philosophy, Happiness and Personal Growth*, New York: Palgrave Macmillan.

Standish, P. (1992), *Beyond the Self*, Brookfield, VT: Avebury.

Standish, P. (1999), "Education without Aims?" in R. Marples (ed.), *The Aims of Education*, 35–49, London: Routledge.

Standish, P. (2011), "Foreword," in D. Bakhurst (ed.), *The Formation of Reason*, x–xii, Malden, MA: Wiley-Blackwell.

Standish, P. (2014), "Bildung, Language, and the Threat to Autonomy," in H. Siegel, "Bildung, the Space of Reasons, and the Educational Aim of Autonomy," *Papers 2014 Philosophy of Education Society of Great Britain Oxford Conference*, 5–6.

Standish, P. (2016), "A Turn in the Conversation," in D. Bakhurst and P. Fairfield (eds.), *Education and Conversation*, 111–26, London: Bloomsbury.

The Enigma of Kaspar Hauser (1974), [Film] Dir. W. Herzog, West Germany: Filmverlag der Autoren.

Todd, S. (2009), *Toward an Imperfect Education: Facing Humanity, Rethinking Cosmopolitanism*, Boulder, CO: Paradigm Publishers.

Tolkien, J. R. R. (1999), *The Silmarillion*, London: HarperCollins.

United Kingdom (1997), "The National Committee of Inquiry into Higher Education," in *Higher Education in the Learning Society: Main Report*, London: Her Majesty's Stationery Office.

United States (1983), *A Nation at Risk: The Imperative for Educational Reform*, Washington, DC: The National Commission on Excellence in Education.

Weekley, E. (1967), *An Etymological Dictionary of Modern English*, vol. 1, Mineola, NY: Dover Publications.

White, J. (1990), *Education and the Good Life: Beyond the National Curriculum*, London: Kogan Page.

White, J. (1999), "In Defence of Liberal Aims in Education," in R. Marples (ed.), *The Aims of Education*, 185–200, London: Routledge.

White, J. (2003), "Five Critical Stances towards Liberal Philosophy of Education in Britain," *Journal of Philosophy of Education*, 37 (1): 147–84.

White, J. (2007), "What Schools Are for and Why," *IMPACT*, 14: 1–51.

Winch, C. (2002), "Strong Autonomy and Education," *Educational Theory*, 52 (1): 27–41.

Winch, C. (2006), *Education, Autonomy and Critical Thinking*, Routledge, New York.

Wittgenstein, L. (1929), "Lecture on Ethics," in L. Wittgenstein (eds.), *Philosophical Occasions*, 37–44, J. C. Klagge and A. Nordmann, Cambridge, MA: Hackett.

Wittgenstein, L. (1958), *Philosophical Investigations*, trans. G. E. M. Anscombe, Oxford: Basil Blackwell.

Wittgenstein, L. (1961), *Notebooks 1914–1916*, trans. and ed. G. E. M. Anscombe, New York: Harper and Brothers.

Wittgenstein, L. (1972), *On Certainty*, trans., ed. G. E. M. Anscombe, New York: Harper and Row.

Wittgenstein, L. (1974), *Philosophical Grammar*, ed. R. Rhees, Oxford: Basil Blackwell.

Wittgenstein, L. (1975), *Philosophical Remarks*, ed. R. Rhees, Oxford: Basil Blackwell.

Wittgenstein, L. (1993), *Philosophical Occasions*, eds. J. C. Klagge and A. Nordmann, Cambridge, MA: Hackett.

Wittgenstein, L. (2007), *Tractatus Logico-Philosophicus*, trans. D. F. Pears and B. F. McGuinness, London: Routledge.

Wittgenstein, L. (2012), *Big Typescript: TS 213*, trans. C. G. Luckhardt and M. Aue, Malden, MA: John Wiley and Sons.

Wood, A. W. (1998), "Hegel on Education," in A. O. Rorty (ed.), *Philosophers on Education*, 300–17, New York: Routledge.

Woodworth, J. L. (2020), "A Letter from the Commissioner of the National Center for Education Statistics," in *The Condition of Education 2020*, Washington, DC: US Department of Education.

Index

achievements. *See also* aims of education; rational aims discourse
    of education 5, 7, 39, 87, 90, 112
    of thinking and being 5
    reality of education's 93–4, 102–5
advent of Being 75, 120, 124, 127, 137, 139
advent of metaphysics 40, 41, 56–9, 72, 120
aims of education. *See also* achievements of education; education; liberal education; new managerialism; rational aims discourse
    as settled 10, 13, 64
    duality of 93–4, 102–3, 104–6
    impasse concerning 92–3
    impossible nature of 98–103
    perenniality of debating 65, 93, 106, 112
    reflection concerning 10–15, 22
    reports on 11–12
    substantiality of 87–93, 97–8
analysis
    higher level of 13, 20, 113
    in philosophy of education 19–21
    of concepts 4, 6, 18
    of language 18, 42
animal. *See also* first and second nature
    behavior 50, 69
    mere 47, 49–51, 54–5, 56
    nonhuman 42, 53–4, 56, 64, 66
    rational 44, 50, 54
    without the rational 51–4
antifoundationalism 13–16, 19, 22, 25–8
application of concepts 18, 21, 42–3
Aristotle 42, 73
at home in the world. *See* being at home in the world
authentic philosophy 2, 14, 22, 25, 39
authority of philosophy 13, 20
autonomy 67, 89–92, 96–8, 104–6, 107 n.3, 108 n.8. *See also* rational freedom; rationality
    rational 91, 97, 105

background of thinking 18, 26, 43, 47–8
Bakhurst, D.
    on autonomy 67, 104–5
    on being at home in the world 64–7
    on embodied mind 50–1, 53
    on philosophy 100
    on rational freedom 93–4
    on space of reasons 49, 137
    on thin teleology 105
    on transformational view 49–51, 53
    on viewing reality 131–2
become what you are 5, 128
becoming
    a thinking being 65, 128
    at home 123
    educated 101
    human 55
    rational 73
    reality 139
Being
    advent of (*see* advent of Being)
    clearing of 52, 76–7
    house of 74–7, 115, 122, 126
    in the midst of 77, 81, 112–13, 121, 125, 127, 138
    unfolding 75–7, 115, 121, 123, 126, 136
being at home in the world 47, 63–8, 72, 77–8, 121–5. *See also* living in language
being-in-the-world. *See* Dasein
Being thinking Being 139
bewitchment 2, 18, 21–2, 26–7, 116
Bildung 47, 60 n.6, 105

Cavell, S. 4
children 5, 29, 41, 59, 69, 81
    feral 55
concept analysis. *See under* analysis
crisis of self-identity 29, 39, 57, 121
critical thinking 80, 94, 103
cultural politics 19–20, 24–5, 39, 49
curriculum 20–2, 64, 88, 92, 98

Dasein 57–8, 73, 75, 115
Dearden, R. 20
deep common accord 1, 26, 129–32, 138
Derrida, J. 4, 121
Descartes, R. 78, 115, 135
différance 121
duality of educational aims. *See* aims of education
dwelling. *See under* Heidegger, *see also* living in language; being at home in the world

education
 administration of 10, 23, 31 n.9 (*see also* new managerialism)
 aims of (*see* aims of education)
 as a leading in 72–4, 76
 as a leading out 72–4, 76–7, 116, 120, 139
 as an orientation to reality 73, 116
 as cultivation 9, 41, 47, 94 102, 105
 as distinctively human 9, 15
 as initiation 47–50, 56, 79–80, 104
 as philosophical 9, 29, 41, 58–9, 132
 as rising to world (*see* world)
 as the advent of metaphysics (*see* advent of metaphysics)
 formal 9, 10 13, 64–5
 ideals of (*see* aims of education)
 integrity of 15–16, 21–3, 25–6, 39
 philosophy of (*see* philosophy of education)
 practical outcomes of 20
 reports on (*see under* aims of education)
 transformational view of 49–51, 54–6, 66
educators. *See* teaching
endless beginning 1, 3–5, 123, 139
environment 39, 45, 51–8, 64, 66. *See also* first and second nature; language; transcendence
etymology 4, 7, 63, 68–74, 81, 114

Fairfield, P. 10
feral children. *See under* children; *see also* first and second nature
finite ends. *See* infinite ends
first and second nature 49–51, 54–6
fishing 44–5, 118
foundationalism. *See* antifoundationalism; fundamental, not foundational

Freud, S. 122
fundamental, not foundational 6, 40–1, 49, 59, 68–72, 122

Gadamer, H.-G.
 Being that can be understood is language 77
 deep common accord (*see* deep common accord)
 on animals 51–4
 on at-homeness 123
 on having a world 66
 on history 69–70, 79–80
 on interpretation 4, 117
 on language and understanding 43–6, 70, 122–3, 125–32
 on listening to language 67–8
 on Nietzsche 124
 on philosophy 46, 80, 116–17, 138
 on rising to world 52–4
 on Wittgenstein 116–17, 138
God
 and Being 75
 and the good 89
 ineffable word of 69
 is dead 136
 name of 136
 philosophy and 100, 122

Heidegger, M.
 on animals 52
 on Being 74–5, 115, 137, 139
 on being-in-the-world 57
 on Dasein (*see* Dasein)
 on dwelling 125
 on existence 73
 on homelessness (*see* homelessness)
 on language 66–7, 71, 75, 111, 119–20, 126–9, 137
 on metaphysics 57–9, 73–4, 120
 on philosophy 57–9, 72–5, 120–1, 135
 on the house of Being 74
 on thinking 72, 120, 135
Hegel, G. W. F. 66, 138
hermeneutical circle 46, 111
hermeneutics 46, 130
hierarchy of sense 45, 64–7, 78
Hirst, P. 20–1, 96–7, 106
historical tradition
 as process 69

Index

as putatively rational inheritance 48
criticism of 78–80
our relationship with 80–1
(*see also* repository of historical mind,
    under language)
historicity
    of etymology 63, 72
    of language 68–72, 75–81, 112, 129
history
    human relationship with 5, 29, 63,
        69–70, 77–81, 113, 119 (*see also*
        historical tradition)
homelessness 122–5, 132
Hume, D. 59 n.1

ideality. *See* aims of education
infinite ends 99–100
initiation. *See under* education; language
instrumentalism 10–15. *See also* new
    managerialism
intellectualism 50, 89, 94, 96
interpretation 25–8, 46, 70, 75, 117–19,
    128–30
    and misinterpretation 2, 65
    responsive nature of 4

Kant, I. 2–3, 9, 55

language
    acquisition of 40, 66, 69, 74
    and reason 3, 44, 135
    and thinking 121
    and thought 43, 46
    artificial 83 n.10
    as a conceptual space 76, 132, 137
    as a house that carries its own
        foundation walls 1, 18, 40, 122, 126,
        139
    as Being that can be understood 77,
        115, 139
    as correspondence 16–17
    as productive 45–6
    as the embodiment of thinking 46–50
    as the fount of reason 48, 71, 126,
        128–9, 137
    as the house of Being (*see under*
        Being)
    as the medium of thought 3, 6, 45
    as the medium of understanding 39,
        43–5, 74, 112

as the repository of historical mind 3,
    46–8, 59, 63, 71–2, 77, 126
as the riverbed of our thoughts 18, 27,
    40, 43, 47–8
call of 3, 132
clearing of 115 (*see also under* Being)
foundations of 3, 18, 71, 116, 122, 126
free universality of 45, 53, 56
incomplete whole of 81, 120, 126, 130,
    136
initiation into 48–9, 56, 80
learning 47–8, 49, 54, 64, 87
limits of 16–17, 115, 129–30, 138
listening to 66–7, 76, 119, 132
literal 70, 78, 81
living in 63, 66–7, 72, 74–7, 111,
    121–6 (*see also* being at home in
    the world)
metaphoric nature of 45–6, 69, 78–9, 81
priority of 63–4, 67–8, 78–81, 127–8,
    130
rough ground of 119–21
resilience of 43, 126, 132
sayings of 120 (*see also under*
    philosophy)
scope of 26–7
shape of 119, 125–32, 137–9
speaking 67, 119, 132
speculative structure of 45, 65
taking care of itself 16–19, 26–8, 42,
    64, 67, 77, 115–16
ubiquity of 44
unfinished 7, 120, 132
unfolding Being (*see under* Being)
untiring universality of 1, 3, 125, 127,
    132
versatility of 43–6, 53–4, 56, 65, 69
liberal education 88–90, 92, 94–9, 104. *See
    also* rational aims discourse
limits
    of meaning 21, 129–30
    of philosophy 28, 90
    of thought 137
London School. *See* Dearden; Hirst;
    Peters

McDowell, J. 47–56, 64–6, 79, 105–6,
    127–8, 132, 138
meaning
    hierarchy of (*see* hierarchy of sense)

infinite possibilities of 65, 70 (*see also under* language)
meaninglessness 12, 17, 135
metaphor. *See under* language; *see also* sense
metaphysics
   advent of 56–9, 64, 72, 120
   as a character of the physical 58
   as nonsense 1–2, 17
   getting under way (*see under* philosophy)
mind. *See also* rationality; rational freedom
   as present in action 50–1
   call of 5, 51

new managerialism 10–15, 22–3
Nietzsche, F. 2, 121, 123–5, 128, 135–6
nihilism 13, 124–5
nothing, the 57–8, 72, 76–7, 112–116, 120–5, 127–8

open question 89, 93, 98–9, 105–6, 112, 121, 128
original language 69

Peters, R. S. 20
phenomenology of language. *See* language; shape of
philosophical theses 1–3, 5–6, 112–14
philosophy
   and true sense 70–2, 112, 114–15, 120
   as a mode of thinking 40
   as conceptual underlaborer 6, 14, 20–1
   as its own antidote 19
   as keeping time 4
   as love of wisdom 9, 29, 80, 101, 105, 113
   as metaphysics' getting under way 59, 120
   as orientation to reality 72, 116
   as parasite 14, 19, 113
   as seeing connections 2
   as self-understanding 29, 40, 63, 123
   as therapy 1–2, 18–19, 22–5, 49, 65, 116
   as thinking about things in general 40–1, 59, 73, 81, 113, 116, 137
   disregards territory 28
   impatience with 100
   mistrust of 2, 14
   of education (*see* philosophy of education)
   responsive nature of 4–5
   tautological sayings of 114–15, 120–1, 135–6
philosophy of education
   analytic approach to 13–14, 20–3
   as cultural politics (*see* cultural politics)
   as therapy (*see under* philosophy)
   literarily crafted 24, 90–1
   mistrust of 14
   skepticism about 9–15
Plato 88–90, 135
policy. *See* aims of education
powers
   of language 63
   of self-movement 42, 53, 55
   of rationality 39, 43–8, 49–56, 94
   of sentience 51, 53, 55
   tripartite distinction of 42, 54–6
practice. *See* theory and practice
pragmatism. *See* Rorty
proto-rationality 54, 69

quietism 1–3, 100. *See also* philosophy as therapy

rational aims discourse 91–8, 104
rational freedom. *See also* aims of education
   as radically underdetermined 98–102
   as the unifying principle of education 102–3
   exhibited in behavior 50–1, 53
   not a standalone aim 102–3
   powers of (*see* powers of rationality)
   transcendental argument for 93–8
rationality. *See also* rational freedom
   principle of (*see* powers)
   proto- (*see* proto-rationality)
reason. *See* aims of education; language; powers; rational freedom; space of reasons
relativism 13, 101
repository of historical mind. *See under* language
returning 111, 116–27, 130–1, 136
revealing 3, 53, 57, 70–2, 115, 122
rising to world. *See under* education
Rödl, S. 42, 54–6, 99–101

romanticism 6, 113–14
Rorty, R. 16, 19, 24, 28, 78–81

same, the 3–5, 114, 119–22, 126–7, 130
same-saying 114–15, 119–20, 124, 129, 131
Scheffler, I. 94–7
science 10–11, 17–24, 42–3, 45–6, 74
second nature. *See* first and second nature
Sellars, W. 28, 40, 47
sense
    and nonsense 1–2, 17, 137
    hierarchy of (*see* hierarchy of sense)
sideways-on 79, 137
Siegel, H. 94–5
silence 16–17, 27, 114–15, 121, 135–6
socio-historical process 48–9, 51, 54–5, 66, 104
Socrates 77, 89, 101
space of reasons 47, 49, 54–6, 65, 76, 137
Standish, P.
    on rational freedom 102, 104
    on the new managerialism 13, 23
    on the rational aims discourse 88–99
subjectivism. *See* relativism
symbiosis 2, 126–9, 132

tautology 114–15, 117–19, 129–30, 132, 136
teaching. *See also* education
    and learning 89–90, 93
    in spite of theory 13–14
    profoundness of 5, 29, 41, 59, 113, 127, 132
theory
    and practice 9–10, 24–8, 64–5
    mistrust of educational (*see under* philosophy of education)
    of education, grand 28, 39
theme 4–5, 112–13
therapy. *See under* philosophy
thin teleology 105
threshold 3, 121–3, 125, 127, 132
tradition. *See* historical tradition
transcendence. *See also* language; nothing, the; transcendental undertaking
    as being beyond beings 57–8
    as being held out into the nothing 57–8, 115, 123
    as climbing beyond 116, 128
    as stepping outside of world history 113
    as transformation 136
    in the *Tractatus* 16–17, 27, 114–15
    occult 50
    of Being 3, 122, 139
    of itself by language 121, 126, 137
    of one's environment 6, 52–3, 57–8, 72, 77, 113, 116
    of one's skin 41
    of the world 124
    thinking as 114–15, 125, 127–8, 132, 135–6
    unheimlich 111, 125–6, 129–32
transcendens pure and simple 74, 77, 115, 120, 128, 139
transcendental
    argument (*see under* rational freedom)
    undertaking 2–3
transformation
    as a character of language 122, 129
    as an effect of philosophy 7, 40, 113–16, 119–22, 129–31, 136
    of metaphysical proportions 3, 39, 49, 56–9, 87
    of monumental proportions 39
transformational view. *See under* education

uncanny 57, 122, 124. *See also unheimlich*
understanding
    and misunderstanding 1–2, 17, 26–7, 45, 80, 116, 130–2
    etymology of 77
ungrounded ground 124
unheimlich 7–8, 121–6, 128–32

White, J. 88–95, 104
Wittgenstein, L.
    on language 1–3, 16–19, 26–7, 41–3, 45–8, 114–21
    on philosophy 1–3, 16–23, 26–9, 114–21

www.ingramcontent.com/pod-product-compliance
Lightning Source LLC
Chambersburg PA
CBHW061841300426
44115CB00013B/2462